Mountain BIKE AMERICA

WASHINGTON BALTIMORE

Second Edition

Illustrations by Michael Drake
Photographs by Scott Adams,
Martín Fernández, Chuck Samuels
Book Design by Gille Collette for Visual Solutions Group

Printed in the United States of America by
Automated Graphic Systems, Inc.

Published by Beachway Press
9201 Beachway Lane
Springfield, VA 22153-1441

10 9 8 7 6 5 4 3 2 1

ISBN 1-882997-06-9

Library of Congress Cataloguing-in-Publication Data
    Adams, Scott; Fernández, Martín
    Mountain Bike America: Washington/Baltimore
    An Atlas of The Washington/Baltimore Area's
    Greatest Off-Road Bicycle Rides / by Scott Adams
    and Martín Fernández
    2nd ed. Springfield, VA: Beachway Press, ©1997.
192 pages: Illustrations, Photographs, Maps, Graphics
1. All-terrain cycling–Washington/Baltimore–Guidebook
Washington/Baltimore–Guidebooks.
97-071745
CIP

BEACHWAY*press*

WASHINGTON BALTIMORE

An Atlas of The Washington/Baltimore
Area's Greatest Off-Road Bicycle Rides

By Scott Adams
Martín Fernández

roduction by Scott Adams, Series Editor

Beachway Press
An addition to
Beachway Press' Mountain Bike America Series

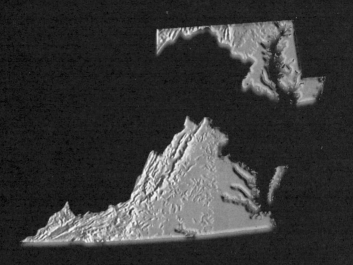

Dear Readers:

*Every effort was made to make
this the most accurate, informative,
and easy-to-use guidebook on the
planet. Any comments, suggestions,
and corrections regarding this
guide are welcome and should be
sent to:*

Beachway Press
c/o Editorial Dept.
9201 Beachway Lane
Springfield, VA 22153

*We'd love to hear from you so
we can make future editions and
future guides even better.*

Thanks and happy trails!

Content

Introduction

The Maps

The Rides

Maryland

Northern Virginia

Washington, DC

Other Places To Ride

Appendix

Index

Preface

TRAIL OBSTACLES: Rocks, Roots, Trees and...Politics?

This guidebook will help you find new trails. Other books on bicycling (and a lot of trial and error) will help you to develop the skills to ride those new trails. Still other books will show you how to fix your bike when you get a flat tire on those trails. But what do you do when your favorite trails get closed to bikes? Well, there's no book to remedy that, really. It all depends on you.

Well, not quite. You see—it *depended* on you. When trails close and bikes are banned, chances are the "problem" had already existed for a while. Maybe a few cyclists had been rolling carelessly past hikers on the trail, frightening them. Or maybe a few cyclists had been riding muddy trails, damaging them. Or maybe the "problem" was that a vocal opponent of mountain bikes had been bending the park management's ear for the past year, worrying them. And finally, because management hadn't heard from bikers, management just gave in.

You see, if some people have their way, mountain bikes will be restricted to pavement, private property, rail trails, and ski resorts in the off-season. Such people often get their understanding of our pastime from sensational television ads or magazine depictions of fearless teenagers engaged in death-defying feats. Sometimes, though, these people form their opinions based on a dangerous experience or a negative encounter on a trail. Fear motivates people. Scare someone today, even by accident, and your trail gets closed tomorrow.

Keeping Trails Open

Trail etiquette is a big part of the answer—the preventive solution. Just ask the International Mountain Bicycling Association (IMBA). Sure, the official IMBA "Rules of the Trail" are important. But simple courtesy, basic caution, and a little empathy for other trail users are the real requirements. In the long haul, they are more important than your bike gear, than your bike clothes—more important even than your bike. After all, a mountain bike isn't very useful if there isn't any place to ride it.

The second simple step to keep trails open is to join together with other cyclists. Join your local mountain bike club or association so your head gets counted and your voice gets heard. Besides, it's often a great way to meet other riders and learn about trails *before* they're published in a book or a magazine. A year's membership rarely costs more than twenty dollars, the cost of a bike tire. You'll find it's well worth it.

MORE

In Maryland, Virginia and Washington, DC, one of the principal mountain bike groups is MORE—the Mid-Atlantic Off-Road Enthusiasts. Around since 1992, MORE is known for keeping trails open. For leading *great* rides. For building new trails and maintaining old ones. For raising money for parks. For educating riders. And, well—for giving mountain bikers a good name. Find out more about MORE from the clubs listing in the back of this book.

Better than Lincoln Logs

And if you think breaking a sweat in the woods on your bike is fun, then working on trails might be more fun than you think. Who needs Erector Sets, Lincoln Logs or Legos, when you can build or maintain a *real* trail? Constructing a new treadway—or fixing an old one—will leave you with a sense of satisfaction that you can't buy in a bike shop. Skeptical? Call MORE and try it once. It's that simple. And it's fun.

IMBA

Speaking of simple, how much did your bike cost? And your helmet? And the bike rack for the car? Add it up, and think about it. Then consider writing out a check for the relatively paltry sum of twenty dollars to the International Mountain Bicycling Association (IMBA). IMBA is *the* national voice for mountain bikers, and twenty dollars gets you membership for a year—and helps support their effort to keep trails and land open to mountain bikers across the nation.

20-20-20

Twenty dollars to your local mountain bike group, twenty dollars to IMBA, and twenty hours a year as a trail volunteer. That's the recipe for access. That's the formula for keeping trails open and healthy. That's the ticket for preserving your fun. You've got the book and the bike. Time to do the rest.

Andy Carruthers

Andy Carruthers is one of the region's most dedicated and vocal mountain bike advocates, working diligently and successfully to keep local trails accessible to cyclists. Many thanks should go to him and all the people he works with to keep our trails alive and in good shape.

Acknowledgment

A special thanks to all the folks who have ever supported my efforts and desires to get to this point. It goes without saying that I would be hard-pressed to manage my ideas and dreams without all of the regular and unending encouragement from those around me and from those who believe in me. Thanks.

Scott Adams

It's hard to embark on a project like this without the help of other people. Thanks to Matt for tagging along and providing a camera, to Peter for riding ahead and scoping out where the trail headed. To Scott for the opportunity, confidence, advice and help. To all the people in the area who bust their butts to keep all of these trails open. To Chris, Wendyll, and everyone at FAT City for my YO. To my viejos. To Miki. And, last but not least, to Cortita for the inspiration, motivation, and support she gives me on a daily basis. Keep the rubber side down, and see you on the trail! Oh, and to Spooky, just because.

Martín Fernández

ntroduction

Introduction

Welcome to the new generation of bicycling! Indeed, the sport has evolved dramatically from the thin-tired, featherweight-frame days of old. The sleek geometry and lightweight frames of racing bicycles, still the heart and soul of bicycling worldwide, have lost much ground in recent years, unpaving the way for the mountain bike, which now accounts for the majority of all bicycle sales in the U.S. And with this change comes a new breed of cyclist, less concerned with smooth roads and long rides, who thrives in places once inaccessible to the mortal road bike.

The mountain bike, with its knobby tread and reinforced frame, takes cyclists to places once unheard of—down rugged mountain trails, through streams of rushing water and thick mud, across the frozen Alaskan tundra, and even to work in the city. There seem to be few limits on what this fat-tired beast can do and where it can take us. Few obstacles stand in its way, few boundaries slow its progress. Except for one—its own success. If trail closure means little to you now, read on and discover how a trail can be here today and gone tomorrow. With so many new off-road cyclists taking to the trails each year, it's no wonder trail access hinges precariously between universal acceptance and complete termination. But a little work on your part can go a long way to preserving trail access for future use. Nothing is more crucial to the survival of mountain biking itself than to read the examples set forth in the following pages and practice their message. Then turn to the maps, pick out your favorite ride, and hit the dirt!

WHAT THIS BOOK IS ABOUT

Within these pages you will find everything you need to know about off-road bicycling in the Washington/Baltimore area. This guidebook begins by exploring the fascinating history of the mountain bike itself, then goes on to discuss everything from the health benefits of off-road cycling to tips and techniques for bicycling over logs and up hills. Also included are the types of clothing to keep you comfortable and in style, essential equipment ideas to keep your rides smooth and trouble-free, and descriptions of off-road terrain to prepare you for the kinds of bumps and bounces you can expect to encounter. The two major provisions of this book, though, are its unique and detailed maps and relentless dedication to trail preservation.

Each of the 33 rides included in this book is accompanied by four very different maps. A *location map* shows where each ride is in relation to the rest of the region; the *profile map* displays an accurate view of each ride's ups and downs, the *route map* leads you through each ride and is accompanied by detailed directions, and a *three-dimensional surface area map* provides a fascinating view of the surrounding topography and landscape.

Without open trails, the maps in this book are virtually useless. Cyclists must learn to be responsible for the trails they use and to share these trails with others. This guidebook addresses such issues as why trail use has become so controversial, what can be done to improve the image of mountain biking, how to have fun and ride responsibly, on-the-spot trail repair techniques, trail maintenance hotlines for each trail, and the worldwide-standard Rules of the Trail.

Each of the 33 rides is complete with maps, trail descriptions and directions, local history, and a quick-reference ride information board including such items as trail-maintenance hotlines, park schedules, costs, and alternative maps. Also included at the end of the book is an "Honorable Mentions" list of alternative off-road rides.

It's important to note that mountain bike rides tend to take longer than road rides because the average speed is often much slower. Average speeds can vary from a climbing pace of three to four miles per hour to 12 to 13 miles per hour on flatter roads and trails. Keep this in mind when planning your trip.

MOUNTAIN BIKE BEGINNINGS

It seems the mountain bike, originally designed for lunatic adventurists bored with straight lines, clean clothes, and smooth tires, has become globally popular in as short a time as it would take to race down a mountain trail.

Like many things of a revolutionary nature, the mountain bike was born on the west coast. But unlike Rollerblades, purple hair, and the peace sign, the concept of the off-road bike cannot be credited solely to the imaginative Californians—they were just the first to make waves.

The design of the first off-road specific bike was based on the geometry of the old Schwinn Excelsior, a one-speed, camel-back cruiser with balloon tires. Joe Breeze was the creator behind it, and in 1977 he built 10 of these "Breezers" for himself and his Marin County, California, friends at $750 apiece—a bargain.

Breeze was a serious competitor in bicycle racing, placing 13th in the 1977 U.S. Road Racing National Championships. After races, he and friends would scour local bike shops hoping to find old bikes they could then restore.

It was the 1941 Schwinn Excelsior, for which Breeze paid just five dollars, that began to shape and change bicycling history forever. After taking the bike home, removing the fenders, oiling the chain, and pumping up the tires, Breeze hit the dirt. He loved it.

His inspiration, while forerunning, was not altogether unique. On the opposite end of the country, nearly 2,500 miles from Marin County, east coast bike bums were also growing restless. More and more old, beat-up clunkers were being restored and modified. These behemoths often weighed as much as 80 pounds and were so reinforced they seemed virtually indestructible. But rides that take just 40 minutes on today's 25-pound featherweights took the steel-toed-boot-and-blue-jean-clad bikers of the late 1970s and early 1980s nearly four hours to complete.

Not until 1981 was it possible to purchase a production mountain bike, but local retailers found these ungainly bicycles difficult to sell and rarely kept them in stock. By 1983, however, mountain bikes were no longer such a fringe item, and large bike manufacturers quickly jumped into the action, producing their own versions of the off-road bike. By the 1990s, the mountain bike had firmly established its place with bicyclists of nearly all ages and abilities, and now command nearly 90 percent of the U.S. bike market.

There are many reasons for the mountain bike's success in becoming the hottest two-wheeled vehicle in the nation. They are much friendlier to the cyclist than traditional road bikes because of their comfortable upright position and shock-absorbing fat tires. And because of the health-conscious, environmentalist movement of the late 1980s and 1990s, people are more activity minded and seek nature on a closer front than paved roads can allow. The mountain bike gives you these things and takes you far away from the daily grind—even if you're only minutes from the city.

MOUNTAIN BIKING INTO SHAPE

If your objective is to get in shape and lose weight, then you're on the right track, because mountain biking is one of the best ways to get started.

One way many of us have lost weight in this sport is the crash-and-burn-it-off method. Picture this: you're speeding uncontrollably down a vertical drop that you realize you shouldn't be on—only after it is too late. Your front wheel lodges into a rut and launches you through endless weeds, trees, and pointy rocks before coming to an abrupt halt in a puddle of thick mud. Surveying the damage, you discover, with the layers of skin, body parts, and lost confidence littering the trail above, that those unwanted pounds have been shed-permanently. Instant weight loss.

There is, of course, a more conventional (and quite a bit less painful) approach to losing weight and gaining fitness on a mountain bike. It's called the workout, and bicycles provide an ideal way to get physical. Take a look at some of the benefits associated with cycling.

Cycling helps you shed pounds without gimmicky diet fads or weight-loss programs. You can explore the countryside and burn nearly 10 to 16 calories per minute or close to 600 to 1,000 calories per hour. Moreover, it's a great way to spend an afternoon.

No less significant than the external and cosmetic changes of your body from riding are the internal changes taking place. Over time, cycling regularly will strengthen your heart as your body grows vast networks of new capillaries to carry blood to all those working muscles. This will, in turn, give your skin a healthier glow. The capacity of your lungs may increase up to 20 percent, and your resting heart rate will drop significantly. The Stanford University School of Medicine reports to the American Heart Association that people can reduce their risk of heart attack by nearly 64 percent if they can burn up to 2,000 calories per week. This is only two to three hours of bike riding!

Recommended for insomnia, hypertension, indigestion, anxiety, and even for recuperation from major heart attacks, bicycling can be an excellent cure-all as well as a great preventive. Cycling just a few hours per week can improve your figure and sleeping habits, give you greater resistance to illness, increase your energy levels, and provide feelings of accomplishment and heightened self-esteem.

BE SAFE—KNOW THE LAW

Occasionally, even the hard-core off-road cyclists will find they have no choice but to ride the pavement. When you are forced to hit the road, it's important for you to know and understand the rules.

Outlined below are a few of the common laws found in Virginia, DC, and Maryland's Vehicle Code book.

- *Bicycles are legally classified as vehicles in the Washington/Baltimore area.* This means that as a bicyclist, you are responsible for obeying the same rules of the road as a driver of a motor vehicle.
- *Bicyclists must ride with the traffic—NOT AGAINST IT!* Because bicycles are considered vehicles, you must ride your bicycle just as you would drive a car—with traffic. Only pedestrians should travel against the flow of traffic.
- *You must obey all traffic signs.* This includes stop signs and stoplights.
- *Always signal your turns.* Most drivers aren't expecting bicyclists to be on the roads, and many drivers would prefer that cyclists stay off the roads altogether. It's important, therefore, to clearly signal your intentions to motorists both in front and behind you.
- *Bicyclists are entitled to the same roads as cars (except controlled-access highways).* Unfortunately, cyclists are rarely given this consideration.
  - *Be a responsible cyclist.* Do not abuse your rights to ride on open roads. Follow the rules and set a good example for all of us as you roll along.

THE MOUNTAIN BIKE CONTROVERSY

Are Mountain Bicyclists Environmental Outlaws?
Do We have the Right to Use Public Trails?

Mountain bikers have long endured the animosity of folks in the backcountry who complain about the consequences of off-road bicycling. Many people believe that the fat tires and knobby tread do unacceptable environmental damage and that our uncontrollable riding habits are a danger to animals and to other trail users. To the contrary, mountain bikes have no more environmental impact than hiking boots or horseshoes. This does not mean, however, that mountain bikes leave no imprint at all. Wherever man treads, there is an impact. By riding responsibly, though, it is possible to leave only a minimum impact—something we all must take care to achieve.

Unfortunately, it is often people of great influence who view the mountain bike as the environment's worst enemy. Consequently, we as mountain bike riders and environmentally concerned citizens must be educators, impressing upon others that we also deserve the right to use these trails. Our responsibilities as bicyclists are no more and no less than any other trail user. We must all take the soft-cycling approach and show that mountain bicyclists are not environmental outlaws.

ETIQUETTE OF MOUNTAIN BIKING

Moving softly across the land means leaving no more than an echo.
Hank Barlow

When discussing mountain biking etiquette, we are in essence discussing the soft-cycling approach. This term, as mentioned previously, describes the art of minimum-impact bicycling and should apply to both the physical and social dimensions of the sport. But make no mistake—it is possible to ride fast and furiously while maintaining the balance of soft-cycling. Here first are a few ways to minimize the physical impact of mountain bike riding.

- *Stay on the trail.* Don't ride around fallen trees or mud holes that block your path. Stop and cross over them. When you come to a vista overlooking a deep valley, don't ride off the trail for a better vantage point. Instead, leave the bike and walk to see the view. Riding off the trail may seem inconsequential when done only once, but soon someone else will follow, then others, and the cumulative results can be catastrophic. Each time you wander from the trail you begin creating a new path, adding one more scar to the earth's surface.

- **Do not disturb the soil.** Follow a line within the trail that will not disturb or damage the soil.
- **Do not ride over soft or wet trails.** After a rain shower or during the thawing season, trails will often resemble muddy, oozing swampland. The best thing to do is stay off the trails altogether. Realistically, however, we're all going to come across some muddy trails we cannot anticipate. Instead of blasting through each section of mud, which may seem both easier and more fun, lift the bike and walk past. Each time a cyclist rides through a soft or muddy section of trail, that part of the trail is permanently damaged. Regardless of the trail's conditions, though, remember always to go over the obstacles across the path, not around them. Stay on the trail.
- **Avoid trails that, for all but God, are considered impassable and impossible.** Don't take a leap of faith down a kamikaze descent on which you will be forced to lock your brakes and skid to the bottom, ripping the ground apart as you go.

Soft-cycling should apply to the social dimensions of the sport as well, since mountain bikers are not the only folks who use the trails. Hikers, equestrians, cross-country skiers, and other outdoors people use many of the same trails and can be easily spooked by a marauding mountain biker tearing through the trees. Be friendly in the forest and give ample warning of your approach.

- **Take out what you bring in.** Don't leave broken bike pieces and banana peels scattered along the trail.
- **Be aware of your surroundings.** Don't use popular hiking trails for race training.
- **Slow down!** Rocketing around blind corners is a sure way to ruin an unsuspecting hiker's day. Consider this—If you fly down a quick singletrack descent at 20 mph, then hit the brakes and slow down to only six mph to pass someone, you're still moving twice as fast as they are!

Like the trails we ride on, the social dimension of mountain biking is very fragile and must be cared for responsibly. We should not want to destroy another person's enjoyment of the outdoors. By riding in the backcountry with caution, control, and responsibility, our presence should be felt positively by other trail users. By adhering to these rules, trail riding—a privilege that can quickly be taken away—will continue to be ours to share.

TRAIL MAINTENANCE

Unfortunately, despite all of the preventive measures taken to avoid trail damage, we're still going to run into many trails requiring attention. Simply put, a lot of hikers, equestrians, and cyclists alike use the same trails—some wear and tear is unavoidable. But like your bike, if you want to use these trails for a long time to come, you must also maintain them.

Trail maintenance and restoration can be accomplished in a variety of ways. One way is for mountain bike clubs to combine efforts with other trail users (i.e. hikers and equestrians) and work closely with land managers to cut new trails or repair existing ones. This not only reinforces to others the commitment cyclists have in caring for and maintaining the land, but also breaks the ice that often separates cyclists from their fellow trailmates. Another good way to help out is to show up on a Saturday morning with a few riding buddies at your favorite off-road domain ready to work. With a good attitude, thick gloves, and the local land manager's supervision, trail repair is fun and very rewarding. It's important, of course, that you arrange a trail-repair outing with the local land manager before you start pounding shovels into the dirt. They can lead you to the most needy sections of trail and instruct you on what repairs should be done and how best to accomplish the task. Perhaps the most effective means of trail maintenance, though, can be done by yourself and while you're riding. Read on.

ON-THE-SPOT QUICK FIX

Most of us, when we're riding, have at one time or another come upon muddy trails or fallen trees blocking our path. We notice that over time the mud gets deeper and the trail gets wider as people go through or around the obstacles. We worry that the problem will become so severe and repairs too difficult that the trail's access may be threatened. We also know that our ambition to do anything about it is greatest at that moment, not after a hot shower and a plate of spaghetti. Here are a few on-the-spot quick fixes you can do that will hopefully correct a problem before it gets out of hand and get you back on your bike within minutes.

- **MUDDY TRAILS.** What do you do when trails develop huge mud holes destined for the EPA's Superfund status? The technique is called corduroying, and it works much like building a pontoon over the mud to support bikes, horses, or hikers as they cross. Corduroy (not the pants) is the term for roads made of logs laid down crosswise. Use small-and medium-sized sticks and lay them side by side across the trail until they cover the length of the muddy section (break the sticks to fit the width of the trail). Press them into the mud with your feet, then lay more on top if needed. Keep adding sticks until the trail is firm. Not only will you stay clean as you cross, but the sticks may soak up some of the water and help the puddle dry. This quick fix may last as long as one month before needing to be redone. And as time goes on, with new layers added to the trail, the soil will grow stronger, thicker, and more resistant to erosion. This whole process may take fewer than five minutes, and you can be on your way, knowing the trail behind you is in good repair.
- **LEAVING THE TRAIL.** What do you do to keep cyclists from cutting corners and leaving the designated trail? The solution is much simpler than you may think. (No, don't hire an off-road police force.) Notice where people are leaving the trail and throw a pile of thick branches or brush along the path, or place logs across the opening to block the way through. There are probably dozens of subtle tricks like these that will manipulate people into staying on the designated trail. If executed well, no one will even notice that the thick branches scattered along the ground in the woods weren't always there. And most folks would probably rather take a moment to hop a log in the trail than get tangled in a web of branches.

- **OBSTACLES IN THE WAY.** If there are large obstacles blocking the trail, try and remove them or push them aside. If you cannot do this by yourself, call the trail maintenance hotline to speak with the land manager of that particular trail and see what can be done.

We must be willing to *sweat for* our trails in order to *sweat on* them. Police yourself and point out to others the significance of trail maintenance. "Sweat Equity," the rewards of continued land use won with a fair share of sweat, pays off when the trail is "up for review" by the land manager and he or she remembers the efforts made by trail-conscious mountain bikers.

RULES OF THE TRAIL

The International Mountain Bicycling Association (IMBA) has developed these guidelines to trail riding. These "Rules of the Trail" are accepted worldwide and will go a long way in keeping trails open. Please respect and follow these rules for everyone's sake.

1. *Ride only on open trails.* Respect trail and road closures (if you're not sure, ask a park or state official first), do not trespass on private property, and obtain permits or authorization if required. Federal and state wilderness areas are off-limits to cycling. Parks and state forests may also have certain trails closed to cycling.

2. *Leave no trace.* Be sensitive to the dirt beneath you. Even on open trails, you should not ride under conditions by which you will leave evidence of your passing, such as on certain soils or shortly after a rainfall. Be sure to observe the different types of soils and trails you're riding on, practicing minimum-impact cycling. Never ride off the trail, don't skid your tires, and be sure to bring out at least as much as you bring in.

3. *Control your bicycle!* Inattention for even one second can cause disaster for yourself or for others. Excessive speed frightens and can injure people, gives mountain biking a bad name, and can result in trail closures.

4. *Always yield.* Let others know you're coming well in advance (a friendly greeting is always good and often appreciated). Show your respect when passing others by slowing to walking speed or stopping altogether, especially in the presence of horses. Horses can be unpredictable, so be very careful. Anticipate that other trail users may be around corners or in blind spots.

5. *Never spook animals.* All animals are spooked by sudden movements, unannounced approaches, or loud noises. Give the animals extra room and time so they can adjust to you. Move slowly or dismount around animals. Running cattle and disturbing wild animals are serious offenses. Leave gates as you find them, or as marked.

6. *Plan ahead.* Know your equipment, your ability, and the area in which you are riding, and plan your trip accordingly. Be self-sufficient at all times, keep your bike in good repair, and carry necessary supplies for changes in weather or other conditions. You can help keep trails open by setting an example of responsible, courteous, and controlled mountain bike riding.

7. *Always wear a helmet when you ride.* For your own safety and protection, a helmet should be worn whenever you are riding your bike. You never know when a tree root or small rock will throw you the wrong way and send you tumbling.

According to Responsible Organized Mountain Pedalers (ROMP) of Campbell, California, "thousands of miles of dirt trails have been closed to mountain bicycling because of the irresponsible riding habits of just a few riders." Don't follow the example of these offending riders. Don't take away trail privileges from thousands of others who work hard each year to keep the backcountry avenues open to us all.

THE NECESSITIES OF CYCLING

When discussing the most important items to have on a bike ride, cyclists generally agree on the following four items.

- **HELMET.** The reasons to wear a helmet should be obvious. Helmets are discussed in more detail in the Be Safe—Wear Your Armor section.

- **WATER.** Without it, cyclists may face dehydration, which may result in dizziness and fatigue. On a warm day, cyclists should drink at least one full bottle during every hour of riding. Remember, it's always good to drink before you feel thirsty—otherwise, it may be too late.

- **CYCLING SHORTS.** These are necessary if you plan to ride your bike more than 20 to 30 minutes. Padded cycling shorts may be the only thing preventing your derriere from serious saddle soreness by ride's end. There are two types of cycling shorts you can buy. Touring shorts are good for people who don't want to look like they're wearing anatomically correct cellophane. These look like regular athletic shorts with pockets, but have built-in padding in the crotch area for protection from chafing and saddle sores. The more popular, traditional cycling shorts are made of skintight material, also with a padded crotch. Whichever style you find most comfortable, cycling shorts are a necessity for long rides.

- **FOOD.** This essential item will keep you rolling. Cycling burns up a lot of calories and is among the few sports in which no one is safe from the "Bonk." Bonking feels like it sounds. Without food in your system, your blood sugar level collapses, and there is no longer any energy in your body. This instantly results in total fatigue and light-headedness. So when you're filling your water bottle, remember to bring along some food. Fruit, energy bars, or some other forms of high-energy food are highly recommended. Candy bars are not, however, because they will deliver a sudden burst of high energy, then let you down soon after, causing you to feel worse than before. Energy bars are available at most bike stores and are similar to candy bars, but provide complex carbohydrate energy and high nutrition rather than the fast-burning simple sugars of candy bars.

BE PREPARED OR DIE

Essential equipment that will keep you from dying alone in the woods:

- **SPARE TUBE**
- **TIRE IRONS**—See the Appendix for instructions on fixing flat tires.
- **PATCH KIT**
- **PUMP**
- **MONEY**—Spare change for emergency calls.
- **SPOKE WRENCH**

- **SPARE SPOKES**—To fit your wheel. Tape these to the chain stay.
- **CHAIN TOOL**
- **ALLEN KEYS**—Bring appropriate sizes to fit your bike.
- **COMPASS**
- **FIRST AID KIT**
- **MATCHES**
- **GUIDEBOOK**—In case all else fails and you must start a fire to survive, this guidebook will serve as excellent fire starter!

To carry these items, you may need a bike bag. A bag mounted in front of the handlebars provides quick access to your belongings, whereas a saddle bag fitted underneath the saddle keeps things out of your way. If you're carrying lots of equipment, you may want to consider a set of panniers. These are much larger and mount on either side of each wheel. Many cyclists, though, prefer not to use a bag at all. They just slip all they need into their jersey pockets, and off they go.

BE SAFE—WEAR YOUR ARMOR

While on the subject of jerseys, it's crucial to discuss the clothing you must wear to be safe, practical, and—if you prefer—stylish. The following is a list of items that will save you from disaster, outfit you comfortably, and most important, keep you looking cool.

- **HELMET**. A helmet is an absolute necessity because it protects your head from complete annihilation. It is the only thing that will not disintegrate into a million pieces after a wicked crash on a descent you shouldn't have been on in the first place. A helmet with a solid exterior shell will also protect your head from sharp or protruding objects. Of course, with a hard-shelled helmet, you can paste several stickers of your favorite bicycle manufacturers all over the outer shell, giving companies even more free advertising for your dollar.
- **SHORTS.** Let's just say Lycra cycling shorts are considered a major safety item if you plan to ride for more than 20 or 30 minutes at a time. As mentioned in The Necessities of Cycling section, cycling shorts are well regarded as the leading cure-all for chafing and saddle sores. The most preventive cycling shorts have padded "chamois" (most chamois is synthetic nowadays) in the crotch area. Of course, if you choose to wear these traditional cycling shorts, it's imperative that they look as if someone spray painted them onto your body.
- **GLOVES.** You may find well-padded cycling gloves invaluable when traveling over rocky trails and gravelly roads for hours on end. Long-fingered gloves may also be useful, as branches, trees, assorted hard objects, and, occasionally, small animals will reach out and whack your knuckles.
- **GLASSES.** Not only do sunglasses give you an imposing presence and make you look cool (both are extremely important), they also protect your eyes from harmful ultraviolet rays, invisible branches, creepy bugs, dirt, and may prevent you from being caught sneaking glances at riders of the opposite sex also wearing skintight, revealing Lycra.
- **SHOES.** Mountain bike shoes should have stiff soles to help make pedaling easier and provide better traction when walking your bike up a trail becomes necessary. Virtually any kind

of good outdoor hiking footwear will work, but specific mountain bike shoes (especially those with inset cleats) are best. It is vital that these shoes look as ugly as humanly possible. Those closest in style to bowling shoes are, of course, the most popular.

- **JERSEY or SHIRT**. Bicycling jerseys are popular because of their snug fit and back pockets. When purchasing a jersey, look for ones that are loaded with bright, blinding, neon logos and manufacturers' names. These loudly decorated billboards are also good for drawing unnecessary attention to yourself just before taking a mean spill while trying to hop a curb. A cotton T-shirt is a good alternative in warm weather, but when the weather turns cold, cotton becomes a chilling substitute for the jersey. Cotton retains moisture and sweat against your body, which may cause you to get the chills and ills on those cold-weather rides.

OH, THOSE CHILLY METROPOLITAN DAYS

If the weather chooses not to cooperate on the day you've set aside for a bike ride, it's helpful to be prepared.

- *Tights or leg warmers.* These are best in temperatures below 55 degrees. Knees are sensitive and can develop all kinds of problems if they get cold. Common problems include tendinitis, bursitis, and arthritis.
  - *Plenty of layers on your upper body:* When the air has a nip in it, layers of clothing will keep the chill away from your chest and help prevent the development of bronchitis. If the air is cool, a polypropylene long-sleeved shirt is best to wear against the skin beneath other layers of clothing. Polypropylene, like wool, wicks away moisture from your skin to keep your body dry. Try to avoid wearing cotton or baggy clothing when the temperature falls. Cotton, as mentioned before, holds moisture like a sponge, and baggy clothing catches cold air and swirls it around your body. Good cold-weather clothing should fit snugly against your body, but not be restrictive.
  - *Wool socks.* Don't pack too many layers under those shoes, though. You may stand the chance of restricting circulation, and your feet will get real cold, real fast.
  - *Thinsulate or Gortex gloves.* We may all agree that there is nothing worse than frozen feet—unless your hands are frozen. A good pair of Thinsulate or Gortex gloves should keep your hands toasty and warm.
- *Hat or helmet on cold days?* Sometimes, when the weather gets really cold and you still want to hit the trails, it's tough to stay warm. We all know that 130 percent of the body's heat escapes through the head (overactive brains, I imagine), so it's important to keep the cranium warm. Ventilated helmets are designed to keep heads cool in the summer heat, but they do little to help keep heads warm during rides in sub-zero temperatures. Cyclists should consider wearing a hat on extremely cold days. Polypropylene Skullcaps are great head and ear warmers that snugly fit over your head beneath the helmet. Head protection is not lost. Another option is a helmet cover that covers those ventilating gaps and helps keep the body heat in. These do not, however, keep your ears warm. Some cyclists will opt for a simple knit cycling cap *sans* the helmet, but these have never been shown to be very good cranium protectors.

All of this clothing can be found at your local bike store, where the staff should be happy to help fit you into the seasons of the year.

TO HAVE OR NOT TO HAVE...
(Other Very Useful Items)

Though mountain biking is relatively new to the cycling scene, there is no shortage of items for you and your bike to make riding better, safer, and easier. I have rummaged through the unending lists and separated the gadgets from the good stuff, coming up with what I believe are items certain to make mountain bike riding easier and more enjoyable.

- **TIRES.** Buying yourself a good pair of knobby tires is the quickest way to enhance the off-road handling capabilities of your bike. There are many types of mountain bike tires on the market. Some are made exclusively for very rugged off-road terrain. These big-knobbed, soft rubber tires virtually stick to the ground with unforgiving traction, but tend to deteriorate quickly on pavement. There are other tires made exclusively for the road. These are called "slicks" and have no tread at all. For the average cyclist, though, a good tire somewhere in the middle of these two extremes should do the trick.

- **TOE CLIPS or CLIPLESS PEDALS.** With these, you will ride with more power. Toe clips attach to your pedals and strap your feet firmly in place, allowing you to exert pressure on the pedals on both the downstroke and the upstroke. They will increase your pedaling efficiency by 30 percent to 50 percent. Clipless pedals, which liberate your feet from the traditional straps and clips, have made toe clips virtually obsolete. Like ski bindings, they attach your shoe directly to the pedal. They are, however, much more expensive than toe clips.

- **BAR ENDS.** These great clamp-on additions to your original straight bar will provide more leverage, an excellent grip for climbing, and a more natural position for your hands. Be aware, however, of the bar end's propensity for hooking trees on fast descents, sending you, the cyclist, airborne.

- **FANNY PACK.** These bags are ideal for carrying keys, extra food, guidebooks, tools, spare tubes, and a cellular phone, in case you need to call for help.

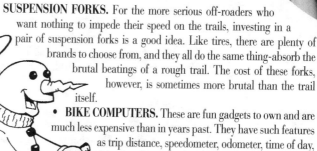

- **SUSPENSION FORKS.** For the more serious off-roaders who want nothing to impede their speed on the trails, investing in a pair of suspension forks is a good idea. Like tires, there are plenty of brands to choose from, and they all do the same thing-absorb the brutal beatings of a rough trail. The cost of these forks, however, is sometimes more brutal than the trail itself.

- **BIKE COMPUTERS.** These are fun gadgets to own and are much less expensive than in years past. They have such features as trip distance, speedometer, odometer, time of day, altitude, alarm, average speed, maximum speed, heart rate, global satellite positioning, etc. Bike computers will come in handy when following these maps or to know just how far you've ridden in the wrong direction.

TYPES OF OFF-ROAD TERRAIN

Before roughing it off road, we may first have to ride the pavement to get to our destination. Please, don't be dismayed. Some of the country's best rides are on the road. Once we get past these smooth-surfaced pathways, though, adventures in dirt await us.

- **RAILS-TO-TRAILS.** Abandoned rail lines are converted into usable public resources for exercising, commuting, or just enjoying nature. Old rails and ties are torn up and a trail, paved or unpaved, is laid along the existing corridor. This completes the cycle from ancient Indian trading routes to railroad corridors and back again to hiking and cycling trails.
- **UNPAVED ROADS.** These are typically found in rural areas and are most often public roads. Be careful when exploring, though, not to ride on someone's unpaved private drive.
  - **FOREST ROADS.** These dirt and gravel roads are used primarily as access to forest land and are kept in good condition. They are almost always open to public use.
    - **SINGLETRACK.** Singletrack can be the most fun on a mountain bike. These trails, with only one track to follow, are often narrow, challenging pathways through the woods. Remember to make sure these trails are open before zipping into the woods. (At the time of this printing, all trails and roads in this guidebook were open to mountain bikes.)
      - **OPEN LAND.** Unless there is a marked trail through a field or open space, you should not plan to ride here. Once one person cuts his or her wheels through a field or meadow, many more are sure to follow, causing irreparable damage to the landscape. "Human tracks are like cancer cells; they spread very quickly."

TECHNIQUES TO SHARPEN YOUR SKILLS

Many of us see ourselves as pure athletes—blessed with power, strength, and endless endurance. However, it may be those with finesse, balance, agility, and grace that get around most quickly on a mountain bike. Although power, strength, and endurance do have their places in mountain biking, these elements don't necessarily form the framework for a champion mountain biker.

The bike should become an extension of your body. Slight shifts in your hips or knees can have remarkable results. Experienced bike handlers seem to flash down technical descents, dashing over obstacles in a smooth and graceful effort as if pirouetting in Swan Lake.

Here are some tips and techniques to help you connect with your bike and float gracefully over the dirt.

Braking

Using your brakes requires using your head, especially when descending. This doesn't mean using your head as a stopping block, but rather to think intelligently. Use your best judgment in terms of how much or how little to squeeze those brake levers.

The more weight a tire is carrying, the more braking power it has. When you're going downhill, your front wheel carries more weight than the rear. Braking with the front brake will help keep you in control without going into a skid. Be careful, though, not to overdo it with the front brakes and accidentally toss yourself over the handlebars. And don't neglect your rear brake!

When descending, shift your weight back over the rear wheel, thus increasing your rear braking power as well. This will balance the power of both brakes and give you maximum control.

Good riders learn just how much of their weight to shift over each wheel and how to apply just enough braking power to each brake, so not to "endo" over the handlebars or skid down a trail.

GOING UPHILL—Climbing Those Treacherous Hills

- *Shift into a low gear (push the thumb shifter away from you).* Before shifting, be sure to ease up on your pedaling so there is not too much pressure on the chain. Find the gear best for you that matches the terrain and steepness of each climb.
- *Stay seated.* Standing out of the saddle is often helpful when climbing steep hills with a road bike, but you may find that on dirt, standing may cause your rear tire to lose its grip and spin out. Climbing requires traction. Stay seated as long as you can, and keep the rear tire digging into the ground. Ascending skyward may prove to be much easier in the saddle.
- *Lean forward.* On very steep hills, the front end may feel unweighted and suddenly pop up. Slide forward on the saddle and lean over the handlebars. This will add more weight to the front wheel and should keep you grounded.
- *Keep pedaling.* On rocky climbs, be sure to keep the pressure on, and don't let up on those pedals! The slower you go through rough trail sections, the harder you will work.

GOING DOWNHILL—
The Real Reason We Get Up in the Morning

- *Shift into the big chainring.* Shifting into the big ring before a bumpy descent will help keep the chain from bouncing off. And should you crash or disengage your leg from the pedal, the chain will cover the teeth of the big ring so they don't bite into your leg.
- *Relax.* Stay loose on the bike, and don't lock your elbows or clench your grip. Your elbows need to bend with the bumps and absorb the shock, while your hands should have a firm but controlled grip on the bars to keep things steady. Steer with your body, allowing your shoulders to guide you through each turn and around each obstacle.
- *Don't oversteer or lose control.* Mountain biking is much like downhill skiing, since you must shift your weight from side to side down narrow, bumpy descents. Your bike will have the tendency to track in the direction you look and follow the slight shifts and leans of your body. You should not think so much about steering, but rather in what direction you wish to go.
- *Rise above the saddle.* When racing down bumpy, technical descents, you should not be sitting on the saddle, but standing on the pedals, allowing your legs and knees to absorb the rocky trail instead of your rear.
- *Drop your saddle.* For steep, technical descents, you may want to drop your saddle three or four inches. This lowers your center of gravity, giving you much more room to bounce around.

- *Keep your pedals parallel to the ground.* The front pedal should be slightly higher so that it doesn't catch on small rocks or logs.
- *Stay focused.* Many descents require your utmost concentration and focus just to reach the bottom. You must notice every groove, every root, every rock, every hole, every bump. You, the bike, and the trail should all become one as you seek singletrack nirvana on your way down the mountain. But if your thoughts wander, however, then so may your bike, and you may instead become one with the trees!

WATCH OUT!
Back-road Obstacles

- **LOGS.** When you want to hop a log, throw your body back, yank up on the handlebars, and pedal forward in one swift motion. This clears the front end of the bike. Then quickly scoot forward and pedal the rear wheel up and over. Keep the forward momentum until you've cleared the log, and by all means, don't hit the brakes, or you may do some interesting acrobatic maneuvers!

  - **ROCKS.** Worse than highway potholes! Stay relaxed, let your elbows and knees absorb the shock, and always continue applying power to your pedals. Staying seated will keep the rear wheel weighted to prevent slipping, and a light front end will help you to respond quickly to each new obstacle. The slower you go, the more time your tires will have to get caught between the grooves.

    - **WATER.** Before crossing a stream or puddle, be sure to first check the depth and bottom surface. There may be an unseen hole or large rock hidden under the water that could wash you up if you're not careful. After you're sure all is safe, hit the water at a good speed, pedal steadily, and allow the bike to steer you through. Once you're across, tap the breaks to squeegee the water off the rims.

    - **LEAVES.** Be careful of wet leaves. These may look pretty, but a trail covered with leaves may cause your wheels to slip out from under you. Leaves are not nearly as unpredictable and dangerous as ice, but they do warrant your attention on a rainy day.

- **MUD.** If you must ride through mud, hit it head on and keep pedaling. You want to part the ooze with your front wheel and get across before it swallows you up. Above all, don't leave the trail to go around the mud. This just widens the path even more and leads to increased trail erosion.

Urban Obstacles

- **CURBS** are fun to jump, but like with logs, be careful.
- **CURBSIDE DRAINS** are typically not a problem for bikes. Just be careful not to get a wheel caught in the grate.
- **DOGS** make great pets, but seem to have it in for bicyclists. If you think you can't outrun a dog that's chasing you, stop and walk your bike out of its territory. A loud yell to *Get!* or *Go home!* often works, as does a sharp squirt from your water bottle right between the eyes.
- **CARS** are tremendously convenient when we're in them, but dodging irate motorists in big automobiles becomes a real hazard when riding a bike. As a cyclist, you must realize most drivers aren't expecting you to be there and often wish you weren't. Stay alert and ride carefully, clearly signaling all of your intentions.
- **POTHOLES**, like grates and back-road canyons, should be avoided. Just because you're on an all-terrain bicycle doesn't mean you're indestructible. Potholes regularly damage rims, pop tires, and sometimes lift unsuspecting cyclists into a spectacular swan dive over the handlebars.

LAST-MINUTE CHECKOVER

Before a ride, it's a good idea to give your bike a once-over to make sure everything is in working order. Begin by checking the air pressure in your tires before each ride to make sure they are properly inflated. Mountain bikes require about 45 to 55 pounds per square inch of air pressure. If your tires are underinflated, there is greater likelihood that the tubes may get pinched on a bump or rock, causing the tire to flat.

Looking over your bike to make sure everything is secure and in its place is the next step. Go through the following checklist before each ride.

- *Pinch the tires to feel for proper inflation.* They should give just a little on the sides, but feel very hard on the treads. If you have a pressure gauge, use that.
- *Check your brakes.* Squeeze the rear brake and roll your bike forward. The rear tire should skid. Next, squeeze the front brake and roll your bike forward. The rear wheel should lift into the air. If this doesn't happen, then your brakes are too loose. Make sure the brake levers don't touch the handlebars when squeezed with full force.
- *Check all quick releases on your bike.* Make sure they are all securely tightened.
- *Lube up.* If your chain squeaks, apply some lubricant.
- *Check your nuts and bolts.* Check the handlebars, saddle, cranks, and pedals to make sure that each is tight and securely fastened to your bike.
- *Check your wheels.* Spin each wheel to see that they spin through the frame and between brake pads freely.
- *Have you got everything?* Make sure you have your spare tube, tire irons patch kit, frame pump, tools, food, water, and guidebook.

The Maps

I don't want anyone, by any means, to feel restricted to just these roads and trails that are mapped. I hope you will have the same adventurous spirit and use these maps as a platform to dive into the Washington/Baltimore area's backcountry and discover new routes for yourself. One of the best ways to begin this is to simply turn the map upside down and ride the course in reverse. The change in perspective is fantastic and the ride should feel quite different. With this in mind, it will be like getting two distinctly different rides on each map.

For your own purposes, you may wish to copy the directions for the course onto a small sheet to help you while riding, or photocopy the map and cue sheet to take with you. These pages can be folded into a bike bag, used with the **BarMap™** or **BarMapOTG™**, or stuffed into a jersey pocket. Please remember to slow or even stop when you want to read the map.

After a short introduction of each particular ride, there will be a profile map, followed by a cue sheet which will provide detailed directions and information about each ride.

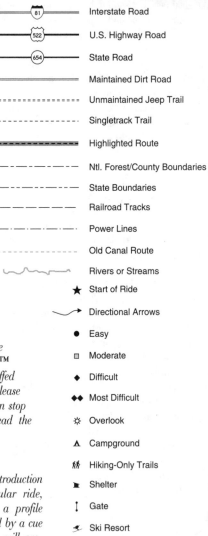

81	Interstate Road
522	U.S. Highway Road
654	State Road
	Maintained Dirt Road
	Unmaintained Jeep Trail
	Singletrack Trail
	Highlighted Route
	Ntl. Forest/County Boundaries
	State Boundaries
	Railroad Tracks
	Power Lines
	Old Canal Route
	Rivers or Streams
★	Start of Ride
	Directional Arrows
●	Easy
▢	Moderate
◆	Difficult
◆◆	Most Difficult
☼	Overlook
▲	Campground
	Hiking-Only Trails
	Shelter
	Gate
	Ski Resort
△	Radio Tower

Ride Location Map

Trails Location

1. Deep Creek Lake State Park
2. New Germany State Park
3. Green Ridge State Forest
4. Greenbrier State Park
5. Gambrill Yellow Trail
6. Catoctin Blue Trail
7. Sugarloaf's Scenic Circuit
8. River Ride
9. Black Hill State Park
10. Schaeffer Farms
11. Seneca Creek State Park
12. Mckeldin Area
13. Avalon Area
14. Northern Central Rail Trail
15. Susquehanna State Park
16. L.F. Cosca State Park
17. Cedarville State Park
18. Patuxent River Park
19. Saint Marys River Park
20. Pocomoke State Park
21. Old Waterford Dirt Ride
22. Ball's Bluff Canal Ride
23. Middleburg Vineyard Tour
24. Great Falls National Park
25. Difficult Run
26. Centreville Power Lines
27. South Run Power Lines
28. Accotink Trail
29. Burke Lake Loop
30. Fountainhead Regional Park
31. Prince William Forest
32. Fort Circle Park
33. C&O Canal

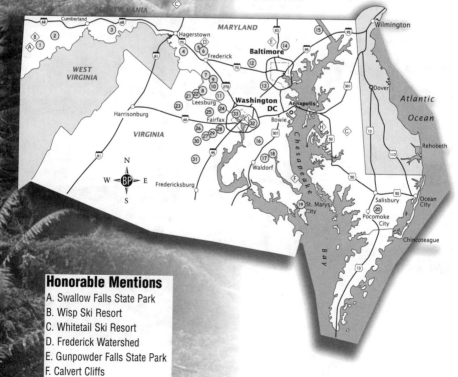

Honorable Mentions

A. Swallow Falls State Park
B. Wisp Ski Resort
C. Whitetail Ski Resort
D. Frederick Watershed
E. Gunpowder Falls State Park
F. Calvert Cliffs
G. Tuckahoe State Park
H. Wye Island
I. Fort DuPont Park

Courses At A Glance

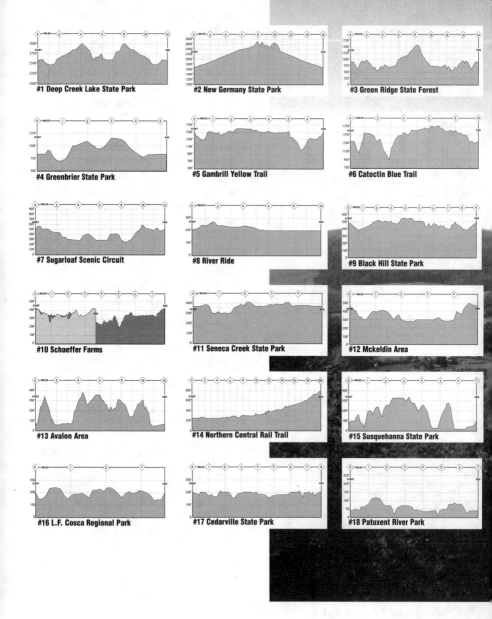

#1 Deep Creek Lake State Park

#2 New Germany State Park

#3 Green Ridge State Forest

#4 Greenbrier State Park

#5 Gambrill Yellow Trail

#6 Catoctin Blue Trail

#7 Sugarloaf Scenic Circuit

#8 River Ride

#9 Black Hill State Park

#10 Schaeffer Farms

#11 Seneca Creek State Park

#12 Mckeldin Area

#13 Avalon Area

#14 Northern Central Rail Trail

#15 Susquehanna State Park

#16 L.F. Cosca Regional Park

#17 Cedarville State Park

#18 Patuxent River Park

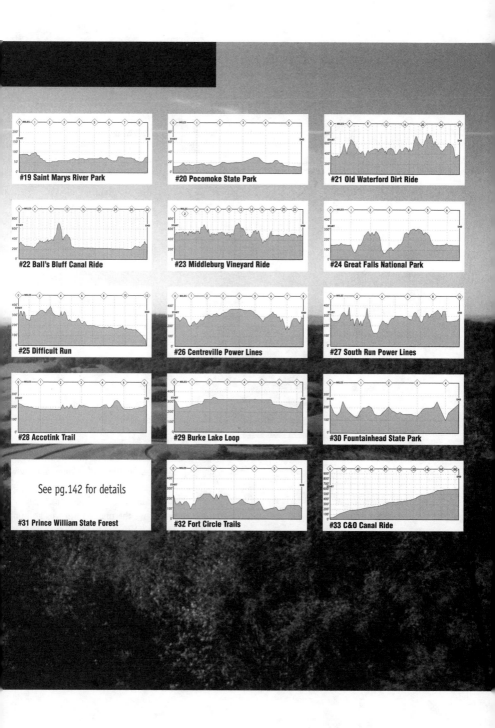

#19 Saint Marys River Park

#20 Pocomoke State Park

#21 Old Waterford Dirt Ride

#22 Ball's Bluff Canal Ride

#23 Middleburg Vineyard Ride

#24 Great Falls National Park

#25 Difficult Run

#26 Centreville Power Lines

#27 South Run Power Lines

#28 Accotink Trail

#29 Burke Lake Loop

#30 Fountainhead State Park

See pg.142 for details

#31 Prince William State Forest

#32 Fort Circle Trails

#33 C&O Canal Ride

How to use the Maps

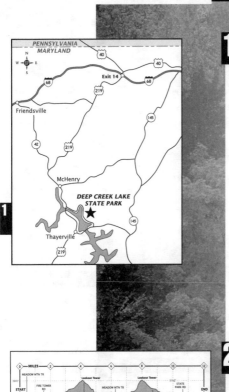

1 Location Map.

This map helps you find your way to the start of each ride from the nearest sizeable town or city. Coupled with the detailed directions at the beginning of the cue, this map should visually lead you to where you need to be for each ride.

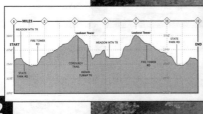

2 Profile Map.

This helpful profile gives you a cross-sectional look at the ride's ups and downs. Elevation is labeled on the left, mileage is indicated on the top. Road and trail names are shown above the map with towns and points of interest labeled in bold.

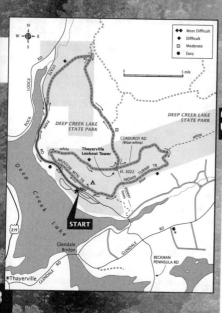

3 Route Map.

This is your primary guide to each ride. It shows all of the accessible roads and trails, points of interest, water, towns, landmarks, and geographical features. It also distinguishes trails from roads, and paved roads from unpaved roads. The selected route is highlighted, and directional arrows point the way.

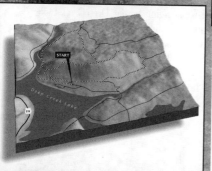

4 3D Surface Area Map.

This three-dimensional look at the earth's surface within the area of the selected ride gives you an accurate representation of the surrounding topography and landscape. The map has been rotated for the best view and includes important roads and trails as well as distinguishable features for points of reference.

Ride Information Board (At the end of each ride section).

This is a small bulletin board with important information concerning each ride.

• The *Trail Maintenance Hotline* is the direct number for the local land managers in charge of all the trails within the selected ride. Use this hotline to *call ahead* for trail access information, or *after your visit* if you see problems with trail erosion, damage, or misuse.

• *Cost.* What money, if any, you may need to carry with you for park entrance fees or tolls.

• *Schedule.* This tells you at what times trails open and close, if on private or park land.

• *Maps.* This is a list of other maps to supplement the maps in this book. They are listed in order from most detailed to most general.

Deep Creek Lake State Park

Start: Meadow Mountain Trail trailhead
Length: 12 miles
Rating: Moderate to Difficult
Terrain: Hilly; forest roads, doubletrack, singletrack
Other Uses: Cross country skiing, flat water canoeing, hiking, hunting, picnic, playground, shelters, snowmobiling, swimming.

Getting There

From **Cumberland**, MD – Take **I-68 west** to **Exit 14** and **Route 219**. Follow Route 219 south through McHenry toward **Thayerville**. Before crossing the main bridge over Deep Creek Lake, turn left on **Rock Ledge Road**. Follow Rock Ledge Road for 2.5 miles, then turn right on **State Park Road**. Continue on State Park Road for 2.5 miles, then turn right on **Waterfront Avenue**. Take an **immediate right**, traveling parallel to State Park Road, and park at the furthermost end of the last parking lot. The trail head is directly across State Park Road.

I f you're interested in traveling to a place with more to offer than just mountain biking, Deep Creek Lake State Park, in the far western panhandle of Maryland's Garret County, may be just the place.

Not only is Deep Creek Lake State Park one of Maryland's premier mountain biking destinations, it is also a favorite vacation spot for people of all interests throughout the Mid-Atlantic. Some of the park's more popular activities aside from mountain biking include cross-country skiing, boating, dining and an array of other outdoor opportunities.

Deep Creek Lake, Maryland's largest inland body of water, was formed by damming the junction of Deep Creek and the Youghiogheny River in 1953. The park officially opened for public use in July, 1959. Today, Deep Creek Lake State Park and Deep Creek Lake are two of Maryland's most popular destinations for outdoor activity.

Famous for its mountains, Garrret County is a prime location for mountain biking in Maryland. There are over 100 miles of trails available for beginning to the most experienced of riders. This ride is intended to be an introduction to Garret County trail riding and includes some of the climbs and views associated with western Maryland's scenic mountain ranges.

A short drive from the West Virginia border, Deep Creek Lake State Park is located just 10 miles northeast of Oakland, Maryland. Currently, the park is accessible only from Rock Ledge Road. However, construction on Glendale Road, the main access road to the park, should be completed by the spring of 1997.

As you enter the park from Rock Ledge Road and State Park Road, pay close attention to the left side and keep your eyes peeled for a sign reading "Meadow Mountain Trail: 50 Yards." This is where your ride begins. Park in the parking lot to your right on the other side of the trees directly across from this sign. If you enter the park from Glendale Road, turn left onto State Park Road, and left again onto

Waterfront Avenue. There will be an immediate right which will lead you into the parking area.

So as not to spend the first mile and a half on paved surface, we start this ride opposite the parking lot at the trail marker and continue into the woods for approximately 50 yards before turning left on Meadow Mountain Trail. This ride primarily follows the white-blazed trail, though it will deviate a bit so that you may end up back at your starting point without too much trouble. Ride parallel to State Park Road for approximately three-quarters of a mile, then pedal the pavement for a quick stretch until you reach Fire Tower Road.

At mile marker 1.5, reach the intersection with Fire Tower Road and State Park Road. Turn right on the dirt road and follow the gradual ascent up the mountain for the next 2.5 miles. When you reach the top, take a break and soak in the view of Deep Creek Lake far below (for best viewing come when the trees are bare). At mile marker 3.9 (the top of the climb) turn left. This is Meadow Mountain Trail. Follow this trail downhill for approximately one mile. This section of singletrack is very unique with a surface not often experienced by cyclists. Because of the trail's swampy nature, park officials have layered a 150-yard section of trail with railroad ties. This section of the trail is known locally as Corduroy Road, and makes for very interesting riding. When you see this, try and imagine the labor that went into laying so many railroad ties side by side!

Reach the intersection of Indian Turnip Trail (blue blazed) at mile marker 4.8 and turn right, continuing downhill along exciting singletrack. Meadow Mountain Trail continues straight at this point. For more information on where straight goes, contact High

MilesDirections

0.0 START at the sign reading "Meadow Mountain Trail 50 Yards."
0.03 Turn left on Meadow Mountain Trail following the white blazes.
0.5 Come to a trail intersection. Continue straight.
0.53 Come to a trail intersection. Turn left and continue downhill towards State Park Road.
0.7 Turn right on State Park Road.
1.5 Turn right on Fire Tower Road. Continue on this dirt road for 2.5 miles uphill to the lookout tower.
3.9 Reach Thayerville Lookout Tower. Turn left at the "T," continuing to follow the white blazes (this portion of trail is blazed both white and blue). Following a short descent, you will reach "Corduroy Road." Continue to the next intersection.
4.8 Turn right at this intersection on Indian Turnip Trail and follow the blue blazes. The white trail continues straight. The blue trail continues downhill through scenic, technical singletrack.
5.2 Turn right, crossing over a wooden bridge. Continue following the blue blazes. The next section of trail levels out and becomes more technical. No dabs allowed!
6.0 Come to an intersection. Turn right.
6.06 Turn right at this intersection and continue uphill, directly beneath the power lines.
6.1 Come to an intersection. Turn left on Meadow Mountain Trail. Continue following the white blazes.

(continues on next page)

MilesDirections *(continued)*

6.2 Come to an intersection. This is where our ride began. Continue straight to complete the rest of this ride.

7.0 Come to an intersection. Continue straight following the white trail blazes. Remain on the white trail until you reach Thayerville Lookout Tower.

8.1 Turn left at this intersection and reach Thayerville Lookout Tower. From here to State Park Road it's 2.5 miles of downhill fire road. Be careful!

10.6 Turn left on State Park Road. Head back to the park.

12.0 Arrive back where you started!

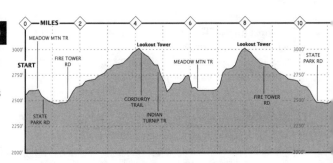

Mountain Sports. They have a great trail guide of the entire area (see *Ride Information* at the end of this chapter).

Our ride continues down the twisty, technical Indian Turnip Trail that takes you back to the base of the mountain. Be careful on this trail, as it is very narrow with plenty of opportunities to unload your bike and hurt your body!

At mile marker 6.0 turn right and continue along the trail beneath the power lines. A short distance later, turn left and head back along Meadow Mountain Trail. Should you continue straight up beneath the power lines, you will end up back at the fire tower. This is not a recommended adventure, however, because of the steep and loose-surfaced ride to the top.

Continue straight following the white blazes of Meadow Mountain Trail. The trail becomes more level and much wider with a pleasant easiness about it. Following this trail to mile marker 6.2 takes you back to the point where your ride began. Should you choose to turn left back to your car and bail out here, you will miss the 2.5-mile descent that whisks you to the

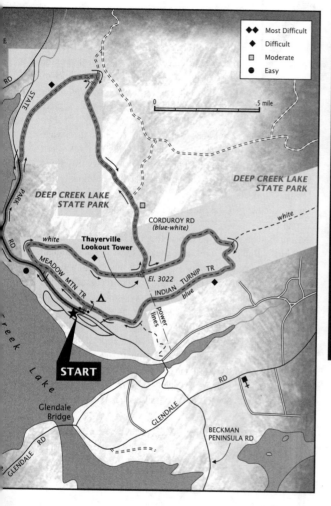

Ride Information

Trail Maintenance Hotline:
Deep Creek Lake State Park
Route 2
Box 69-C
Swanton, MD 21561
(301) 387-5563

Schedule:
Day Use
8 a.m. to sunset

Bike Shop/trail information:
High Mountain Sports
P.O. Box 85
McHenry, MD 21541
(301) 387-4199

Maps:
USGS maps: McHenry, MD
Delorme: Maryland/Delaware Atlas
& Gazetteer – Page 65 C-6

completion of this ride. Keep this in mind and consider your choices carefully! If you choose to finish the ride in its entirety, continue straight, following the white blazes. You will again head toward the fire tower, climbing up to the top of the mountain. At mile marker 8.1, reach the top of the climb and the fire tower, grab one last glimpse of this great view, then turn left and descend for 2.5 miles of downhill adventure!

At the bottom of the descent, turn left on State Park Road and continue back to the parking lot and your car.

New Germany State Park

Start: Poplar Lick Run ORV Trail Parking (Big Run State Park)
Length: 16 miles
Rating: Easy to Moderate
Terrain: Wet; dirt roads, doubletrack, singletrack
Other Uses: Hiking, ORV, cross country skiing, camping

Getting There

From **Cumberland** – Take **I-68 west** to **Exit 24**. Follow signs to **New Germany/ Savage River State Forest**. Continue 4 miles past the New Germany State Park entrance on **New Germany Road** and turn left onto **Big Run Road**. Continue straight on Big Run Road for approximately four miles and turn left on **Savage River Road**. Follow this Savage River Road for another four miles and turn left on **Poplar Lick Run Off Road Vehicle Road**. Park immediately to the left. The ride begins here.

New Germany State Park and Big Run State Park both lie within the 52,800-acre Savage River State Forest, the largest of Maryland's state forests. Our ride covers only a small portion of this vast wilderness area and the possibilities of other equally great rides are numerous. Detailed maps and directions can be obtained from Forest Headquarters, as well as information regarding sensitive and restricted areas.

Savage River State Forest is the birthplace of both the Savage and Casselman Rivers. Lying on opposite sides of the Eastern Divide, the two rivers flow in opposite directions; the Savage River running south into the Chesapeake Bay and eventually the Atlantic, and the Casselman River flowing north into the Youghiogheny, then the Mississippi, and ultimately the Gulf of Mexico.

Your ride begins on the Poplar Run Off Road Vehicle (ORV) Trail in Big Run State Park and works its way to the mountain biking trails of New Germany State Park. A mixture of moderate climbing, singletrack and doubletrack, and dirt roads make this a wonderfully varied ride. After parking, ride straight through the first of several creek crossings. It's recommended you make this ride during warm spring and summer days, because you will more than likely get very wet. Ride on this road for approximately five miles, the majority of which will all be uphill. The grade, however, is not very significant, so don't be too worried. Stay on guard, though, because this area does allow motorized vehicles and you may occasionally have to share the trails with a four-wheel drive.

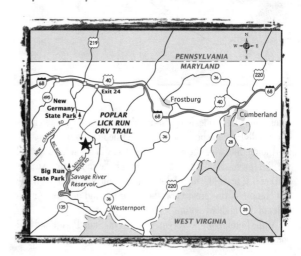

MilesDirections

0.0 START from the Poplar Lick Run ORV parking area an head towards the creek. You must immediately make the first of several creek crossings. Follow Poplar Lick Run ORV Trail, a gravel/dirt road, for approximately five miles.

5.1 After a five-mile gradual ascent, turn right and pedal through the gate, continuing straight on the blue trail.

5.8 Bear left and continue on the green trail.

5.9 Immediately after crossing the bridge, turn left on the yellow trail. Follow the yellow blazes to the left.

6.5 After a short, steep downhill, turn left, continuing to follow the yellow blazes. The trail to the right is also blazed yellow. This branch of the trail will take you back towards the small bridge you crossed earlier.

6.6 Make a ninety-degree turn to the right and continue straight toward the green trail. Turn left at the green trail.

6.7 Continue straight on the green trail.

7.0 Bear left over the wooden bridge.

7.1 Turn right on the park road, then bear right at the "Y" intersection (by the phone booth), heading toward the amphitheater. Parking Lot #5 is to the right. This is where all trails in New Germany State Park begin. If you would like to ride trails not included in this ride, come back, study the trail map and go for a few extra miles.

(continues on next page)

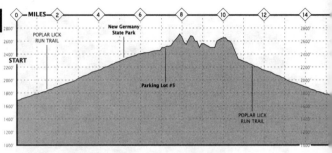

MilesDirections *(continued)*

7.3 Turn right at this road. The red trailhead is immediately to your left. Continue on the red trail for approximately half a mile, at which point the trail will level out and treat you to a short but fast downhill.

8.1 Turn left onto the light blue trail. Notice the one-way sign on the red trail.

8.6 Continue straight on the blue trail.

9.0 Turn left following the green blazes.

9.6 Turn left following the blue blazes.

9.7 Turn right continuing to follow the blue blazes. Don't go beyond the gate and the "No Jeep" sign unless you are confident of your backcountry skills.

Information on this trail is available at New Germany State Park Headquarters on New Germany Road.

(continues on next page)

When you reach mile marker 5.1, turn right and go through a gate. This marks the entrance to New Germany State Park. The next four miles are spent on a variety of exciting singletrack and doubletrack trails.

To proceed, enter the park's forest directly ahead of the gate and follow the blue blazes, making sure the creek is on your right. Approximately three-quarters of a mile later, bear left and follow the green blazes. At this point, you are at the center of New Germany State Park's trail system. As great as these trails are they, unfortunately, only cover a small section of the park. Following any of the clearly marked trails will always keep you within two to three miles of New Germany's Parking Lot #5, the starting point for all of the trails within the park.

Turn left and cross over a small wooden bridge and begin following what is now a yellow-blazed trail. This is a fun section of singletrack that culminates in approximately three-quarters of a mile with a short steep descent. At mile marker 6.5, turn left, continuing to follow the yellow blazes. The trail to the right is also blazed yellow and, if you follow it, you will end up where you got on the yellow trail in the first place. If you enjoyed that last section, turn right here and do this small yellow-blazed loop again.

Continue straight on the green trail until you reach the road and the lake. This 13-acre lake was formed many years ago when Poplar Lick Run was dammed for mill operations. Today the lake is a popular swimming hole and picnic area. Feel free to take a break from riding and jump in for a swim. You can also rent rowboats for a quick sail or simply hang out by the water and cool off your feet. When you're ready to move on, turn right and head up the road. To your right is Parking Lot #5 and New Germany State Park's main

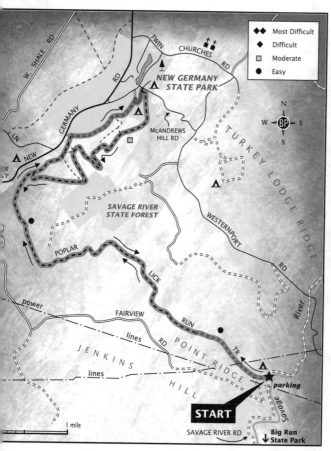

◆◆	Most Difficult
◆	Difficult
▢	Moderate
●	Easy

NEW GERMANY STATE PARK

McANDREWS HILL RD

TWIN CHURCHES RD

W. SHALE RD

GERMANY RD

TURKEY LODGE RIDGE

SAVAGE RIVER STATE FOREST

WESTERNPORT RD

POPLAR

LICK

RUN

FAIRVIEW RD

power lines

JENKINS

lines

HILL

POINT RIDGE TR

parking

START

SAVAGE RIVER RD

Big Run State Park

1 mile

Ride Information

Trail Maintenance Hotline:
New Germany State Park
349 Headquarters Lane
Grantsville, MD 21536
(301) 895-5453

Schedule:
Open from dawn til dusk,
year-round

Maps:
USGS maps: Bittinger, MD; Barton,
MD; Grantsville, MD; Avilton, MD
DeLorme: Maryland/Delaware Atlas
& Gazetteer – Page 62 B-2

MilesDirections (continued)

9.8 Continue straight at this intersection staying on the blue trail. Prepare yourself for a big-ring descent. It's all downhill from here! *Yee Haa! What a descent!*

10.7 Turn left through the yellow gate, then left and downhill. You're back on Poplar Lick Run ORV Trail. Continue straight for the next 5.1 miles on this trail back toward Savage River Road.

15.8 Arrive back where you began this ride. Drive back to New Germany State Park and park in Parking Lot # 5 where all the park's trails start. Try some of the ones we didn't cover in this loop.

trailhead. Continue up the road then bear right toward the amphitheater. A short distance later you will turn left, then left again onto a clearly marked red-blazed trail. Continue along the red-blazed trail for approximately three-quarters of a mile before turning left onto the light blue trail (notice the one-way sign on the red trail).

Continue on the light blue trail which eventually merges with the green trail and later the dark blue trail. At mile marker 9.8 you will have reached the top of the ascent. The ride is all downhill from here to your car. Turn right and get ready for a big-ring descent! Follow the blue blazes until you reach the gate. Turn left and follow Poplar Lick Run ORV Trail all the way down to your car. Five fun-filled downhill miles later and you're back to the beginning of this ride.

Green Ridge State Forest

Ride Specs

Start: Green Ridge State Forest Headquarters
Length: 15.6 miles
Rating: Moderate to Difficult
Terrain: Hilly; forest roads, doubletrack, singletrack
Other Uses: Boat launch, primitive camping, fishing, flat water canoeing, hiking, hunting, picnicking, horseback, shooting range, snowmobiling, visitors center.

Getting There

From **Hagerstown**, MD –
Take **I-68 west** to **Sideling Hill**. 10 miles west of Sideling Hill, exit onto **M.V. Smith Road** and **Green Ridge State Forest (Exit 64)**. Follow the signs to **Green Ridge State Forest Headquarters**. Your ride will begin there.

G reen Ridge State Forest, in east Allegany County, is a vast 40,000-acre forest stretching across the rugged mountains of Western Maryland. The forest boasts over 100 remote camping sites, over 22 miles of trails, and more than 200 miles of forest roads on which to ride, making it an ideal getaway for avid cyclists and campers alike. Home also to the Maryland National Mountain Bike Championship, Green Ridge State Forest is fast becoming a destination for Washington, DC, and Baltimore riders. Our ride takes you up and down many of the forest roads and singletrack trails that made up the Expert and Sport course of the 1996 race, giving cyclists a little taste of what the racers had to endure.

The ride begins at the forest headquarters. Take a moment to walk to the overlook opposite the parking lot on the other side of the building and take a peak at the terrain over which you will be riding. Make sure to bring plenty of water and be prepared for a rollercoaster ride through the forest.

To begin, ride away from the forest headquarters and turn right on M.V. Smith Road, the first part of which is a fast descent. Soon after the pavement ends you will be greeted by a wide dirt road and a sign welcoming you into the forest.

After a small creek crossing at the bottom of the descent, turn left heading uphill on Catpoint Road. If you reached Fifteenmile Creek, you've gone too far. As you reach the top of this climb, you may begin to hear sounds of Interstate-68 straight ahead. Before crossing beneath I-68, turn right on Mountain Road, which changes to dirt rather quickly. Follow the steel cable railing on the right. As soon as the cable railing ends just before Mountain Road curves to the right, turn right into the woods on a singletrack trail called Adams Road. Pay close attention, because this trailhead is well hidden. For the next mile and a half you will be cruising down-

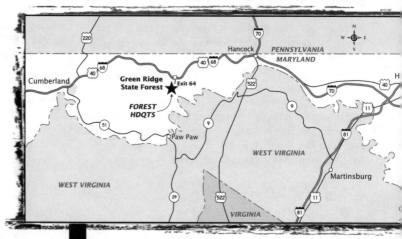

MilesDirections

0.0 START from Forest Headquarters parking lot and head toward M.V. Smith Road.

0.1 Turn right on M.V. Smith Road.

0.9 Turn left immediately after a small creek crossing on Catpoint Road. Start climbing!

1.3 How do your legs feel?

1.6 Turn right at this intersection on Mountain Road. I-68 will be to your left.

2.0 Approximately 10 yards after the steel cable railing on your right ends, turn right on a singletrack trail into the woods called Adams Road. Keep your eyes pealed for this trailhead. It's easy to miss. If Mountain Road curves to the right away from I-68, you've gone too far. Immediately after you enter the singletrack, turn right and follow the trail downhill, paralleling Mountain Road.

3.6 Turn right at this intersection. Downhills like that last one make climbing a bit easier to endure!

3.8 The trail continues across the creek. Look for the white diamond blazes marking the trail.

4.35 The trail turns sharply left, away from the creek. Get ready for a short steep climb.

4.6 Come out into a large clearing in the forest. The trail continues straight ahead. Look for the tree with a white diamond blaze.

5.5 Reached the intersection of Adams Road and Dug Hill Road. Turn left and continue up Dug Hill Road.

hill through the forest along some great Maryland singletrack.

At mile marker 3.6 turn right, traveling parallel to the creek off to your left. You will soon be crossing this creek and your feet are certain to get wet. Once across the creek the trail is marked with white diamonds. At mile marker 4.6, reach an opening in the forest, continue following the white blazes down a short descent, and end up at the intersection of Adams Road and Dug Hill Road. Turn left here and continue uphill for the next two miles toward the intersection of Dug Hill Road and Stafford Trail.

Turn right on Stafford Trail and continue uphill for one more mile—all this climbing will soon pay off. Look to your right as you ride up Stafford Trail. You may be able to witness some great views of the Potomac River meandering off in the distance through the forest below. In the fall you will be treated to a spectacular array of colors comparable only to those found in New England.

(continues on next page)

MilesDirections *(continued)*

7.2 Approximately one tenth of a mile after Campsite 49E, turn right on Stafford Trail. This intersection should be clearly marked. Still climbing.

8.3 Reach the intersection of Stafford Trail and Stafford Road. Our ride takes us to the right, continuing along Stafford Trail. The longer version of the Maryland State Mountain Bike Championship race continues to the left. More information on this ride can be obtained from park headquarters.

8.6 Immediately to your right is an overlook from which you can see Big Ridge and the Potomac River. Continue straight.

8.8 Pay attention! The Stafford Road turns sharply left. Turn right at this point into the woods along a singletrack trail. A series of steep singletrack switchbacks leads you down the mountain. Be careful, pay attention, and pick a good line. If you pass the entrance to Campsite 48E, you missed this turn.

(continues on next page)

At mile marker 8.6 reach Stafford Road and the end of the climb. Turn right and continue down this road. Immediately after making this turn, there is an overlook off to your right. Stop and take a break here and gather your wit. The following downhill section will require all your senses to be tuned in and in check. Continue on your way; pay close attention to the right for the trail. As soon as Stafford Road curves sharply to the left, you need to turn right into the woods on the singletrack trail. If you're lucky, the trail will be marked by a leftover race marker, but don't count on it. If you miss this turn and reach campsite #48E, you've gone too far.

What follows on this trail is some serious downhill singletrack with a series of switchbacks designed to test all your bike handling skills. Be careful and don't get in over your head—figuratively or literally! After approximately one mile of this, you reach the end of the descent and connect with Dug Hill Road. Continue straight down along the road for about a half-mile until you reach the intersection with Adams Road. If you'd like, continue straight at this intersection and do it all over again. Or, like most sane people, turn left and return along Adams Road, crossing the creek, then back up Mountain Road to Catpoint Road and M.V. Smith Road.

All in all, this loop is about 16 miles of climbs and descents. By studying maps provided by the state forest, you could ride a far longer course. But unless your back-country skills are extraordinary and you plan to spend the night in the forest, stick to this ride for now. Come back another day to tackle the rest of Green Ridge State Forest's 200 miles of dirt roads and trails.

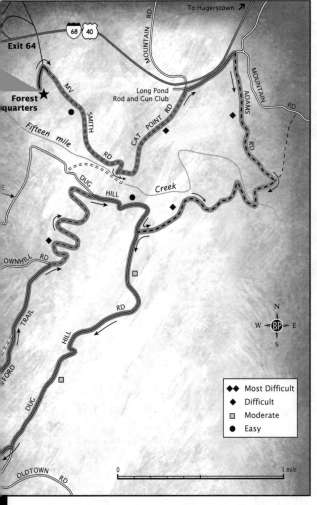

Most Difficult ◆◆
Difficult ◆
Moderate ◻
Easy ●

Ride Information

Trail Maintenance Hotline:
Green Ridge State Forest
Headquarters
28700 Headquarters Dr NE
Flintstone, MD 21530
(301) 478-3124

Schedule:
Open from dawn til dusk,
year-round

Maps:
USGS maps: Artemas, MD;
    Paw Paw, MD
DeLorme: Maryland/Delaware Atlas
    & Gazetteer – Page 68-69 B-3

MilesDirections (continued)

9.8 Continue straight (bear right) at this intersection with Dug Hill Road.

10.3 Reach the intersection of Dug Hill Road and Adams Road again. It's time to backtrack the first 5.5 miles of your ride.

12.0 Cross the creek again and get wet. Continue straight on the other side.

12.2 Turn left at this intersection. It's time to head straight back up this hill to the top.

13.5 Turn left and continue up Mountain Road for three tenths of a mile.

13.8 Turn left on Catpoint Road, continuing downhill toward M.V. Smith Road. The next three-quarters of a mile treats you to the final downhill of the ride.

14.5 Turn right at this intersection and get ready for the final uphill of the ride.

15.4 Turn left at this intersection and continue straight to your car.

15.6 Reach the car.

• East of Green Ridge State Forest is one of northeastern United States' greatest rock exposures called Sideling Hill. If you've got the time, a short visit to this massive road-cut rock exposure could prove an excellent lesson in geology.

• If you're thirsty for a cold brew after the ride, visit Bill's Place in Little Orleans, off Orleans Road (Exit 62 off I-68). They'd be glad to fix you up with some delicious beverages. Bill's Place is also accessible from the C&O Canal. So if you're on your way to Cumberland along the canal, stop in for a bite to eat.

• Green Ridge State Forest is a remote area especially popular among hunters. Take every precaution to ensure that your visit is enjoyable and safe. Call the Forest Headquarters for hunting season schedules and information.

Greenbrier State Park

Start: Beach/lake parking lot
Length: 5.2 miles
Rating: Moderate to Difficult
Terrain: Rocky singletrack; doubletrack and fireroads

G reenbrier State Park, 10 miles east of Hagerstown along Route 40, is both rich in history and a great place to ride.

Nestled in the scenic Appalachian Mountains, one of the world's oldest mountain ranges, Greenbrier was once a popular area for fur trapping, trading, exploration, and farming. Early in its history, small farms settled into the fertile river valleys and today's surrounding roads still follow much of the same layout of those early industrious pioneers. As you ride along the park's many scenic trails, pay close attention to your surroundings, as evidence of foundations from old farmhouses, once thriving iron furnaces, and ruins of old log cabins still exist. The singular and distinctive flat circular shapes of hearths where charcoal was made to fuel these old iron furnaces are scattered throughout the area as well.

Because of its unique history, 1,200 acres of woodlands, 42-acre man-made lake, and miles of mountainous trails, Greenbrier State Park has become one of Maryland's most popular recreational parks and has most recently begun hosting races for the Maryland Mountain Bike Point Series.

Greenbrier State Park is also in close proximity to some other great off-road riding areas. If you are traveling west, you should definitely stop at Green Ridge State Forest, home of the Maryland State Mountain Bike Championship, and experience their vast 40,000-acre forest of trails. Farther west is Deep Creek Lake State Park. Southeast a bit is Gambrill State Park, boasting, unquestionably, some of the east coast's greatest singletrack, with over 18 miles of trails, including a section of the famed Catoctin Mountain Trail.

From **Washington** – Take Route **270 north** to **Route 40 west.** Follow Route 40 for approximately 11 miles. **Greenbrier State Park** entrance is on your left. Continue straight, parking at the lake parking lot.
Fees: $2.00 per person (well worth it!)

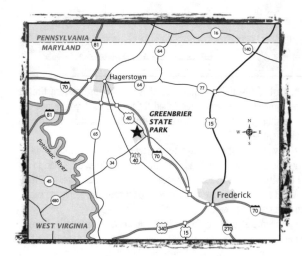

MilesDirections

0.0 START at the parking lot and head to the other side of the lake from the boat launch. Once you cross to the opposite side of the lake, enter the woods at the trailhead marked "Orienteering Trail."

0.3 Bear right (straight) at this intersection and continue downhill.

0.8 Turn left at the gravel road.

1.1 Turn right off the gravel road onto the singletrack trail and continue right. Follow the white blazes, riding away from the trail marked "Rock Oak Fire Trail."

1.2 Continue straight (right) immediately after crossing the creek.

1.4 Turn left at this intersection and follow the white blazes up the mountain.

1.7 Bear right and continue uphill. You have just come out of the "Kettle Mountain Fire Trail."

1.9 Bear left and follow the "Hickory Ridge Fire Trail" sign.

2.0 Turn right at this trail intersection and get ready for a series of off-camber technical sections. This is a challenging section of trail that will test your balance and stamina.

2.9 Turn right at this trail section, then immediately left, heading back in the direction from which you just came.

3.1 Turn right at this intersection and get ready for a short, fast descent that drops you into a small rock garden then immediately sends you back up a rocky technical ascent.

3.3 Turn right at this trail intersection.

(continues on next page)

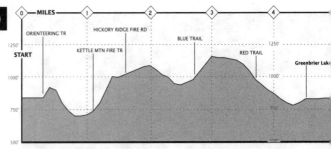

MilesDirections *(continued)*

3.4 Turn left at this trail intersection, following the blue blazes, and get ready for a one-mile gradual climb.

4.0 Continue straight, heading downhill toward the lake for approximately one mile. This is a fast descent so pay attention and be ready to slow down quickly. This section of trail is closest to the lake and used by a lot of hikers.

4.8 Reach an opening with the lake to your right. At this point you can see the parking lot on the other side of the lake. Continue straight riding parallel to the lake.

5.0 Bear left on the fire road, away from the lake.

5.1 If you choose to ride the loop again, turn left. After a short downhill, this trail will put you at mile marker 0.3. If not, bear right and continue toward the "Orienteering Trail" trailhead.

5.2 Reach the "Orienteering Trail" trailhead. Travel to the other side of the lake on the grass toward the boat launch. You may also continue straight along the fire road. This also takes you to the boat launch.

Your ride here at Greenbrier begins at the parking lot directly above the lake. Start by pedaling to the other side of the lake along the grassy area on the northern edge. When you reach the sign marked "Orienteering Trail" the real ride begins. There are approximately 12 miles of trails in Greenbrier State Park. This ride covers only about five and a half of those miles, leaving quite a bit left over for you to discover yourself.

Start out on the white trail, crossing over the first of a handful of hills in the first three-quarters of a mile. Enjoy this descent because the next part of the ride will mostly be up a steady climb up to the ridge. At mile marker 0.8, turn left on a coarse gravel road. You will be on this road for just three-quarters of a mile before turning right onto more singletrack, continuing to follow the white blazes. At this right turn, be sure to ride away from the "Rock Oak Fire Trail." Cross a small creek and continue along the white-blazed trail. The white blazes connect three of the park's main trails; the Hickory Ridge Trail, the Snelling Fire Trail, and the Mountain Fire Trail. You are currently on the Mountain Fire Trail heading to the Hickory Ridge Trail.

At mile marker 2.0, you will have reached the end of your climb. Prepare for a series of technical off-camber sections of east coast singletrack at its best. This section is fun and challenging and will surely test your balance and stamina. Just remember that momentum is your friend. Pedaling too slowly along this trail may allow the singletrack to have its way with you.

After a series of short ascents and one great downhill that empties you into a wonderful rock garden, you will intersect with the white and blue trails. Turn left and continue on the blue trail. This turn will lead you uphill for

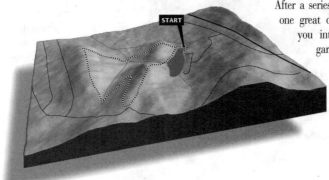

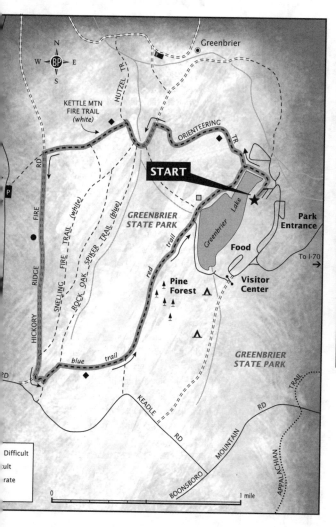

Ride Information

Trail Maintenance Hotline:
South Mountain Recreation Area
21843 National Pike (Route 40)
Boonsboro, MD 21713
(301) 791-4767

Schedule:
Open year-round
Camping quiet hours are from
11 p.m. to 7 a.m.

Maps:
USGS maps: Funkstown, MD;
    Myersville, MD
Delorme: Maryland/Delaware Atlas
    & Gazetteer – Page 71 C-6
Greenbrier State Park trail map

one mile to the top of the ridge. The ascent is gradual and slow, but is rewarded with a fast, loose-terrained descent that will bring you back to the lake. This is a very popular trail because of its proximity to the lake.

At mile marker 4.8, reach the lake. Continue riding with the lake on your right. If you choose, you can head left and pick up the fire road that initially took you to the white trail. If you look hard, you may see the trailhead to your left at the bottom of the hill. At this point, your car should be clearly visible at the other side of the lake.

If you're up to it, go for another loop. If not, head on back to the beaches at the other side of the lake and relax under the sun.

Gambrill Yellow Trail

Ride Specs

Start: High Knob Scenic Area parking lot
Length: 6.5 miles
Rating: Difficult
Terrain: Rocky singletrack

Six miles northwest of Frederick, Maryland, on Catoctin Mountain is Gambrill State Park—a jewel for mountain bikers. Named for the late James H. Gambrill, Jr. of Frederick, the park had its beginnings when spirited conservationists bought the land on the mountain and donated it to the city of Frederick. In September of 1934, the park was presented to the state, and since then has been used as a recreational favorite.

The Yellow Trail, at 6.5 miles, is the longest loop in the Gambrill trail system and the perfect trail for up-and-coming mountain bikers. Your ride starts with a fast descent paralleling Gambrill Park Road. By the time you reach the main trail parking lot, you will have had a fair sampling of what's to come.

From the parking lot, cross the street and head back into the woods toward the first grueling climb. Once at the top, take the chance to enjoy some of the breathtaking views of Middletown Valley, southwest of the mountain. Soon after the overlooks, hook up with the Black Trail. Had enough? You can bail out here by turning right and heading up the hill to Gambrill Park Road—the point where the ride began. If you wish to go on, continue straight, following the Yellow/Black Trail.

The terrain changes slightly as you catch quick glimpses of Middletown Valley through the trees on your left. Continue following the Yellow/Black blazes up a short technical hill to a divide. You'll want to veer left. The Black Trail splits to the right and back toward the High Knob area. After a short ascent, begin a gradual descent that, in a matter of moments, becomes covered with large menacing rocks, making your advance much more dif-

Getting There

From **Washington** – Take **Route 270 North** to **Route 40 west**, Turn **right** on **Gambrill Park Road**, enter the park, pass the parking lot on your right and continue to the "T" intersection. Go **left** to the **High Knob Scenic Area** and park in the first lot on your left directly across from the swings.

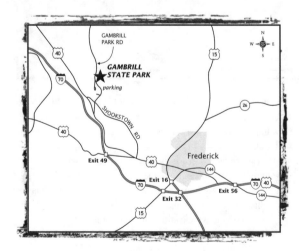

MilesDirections

0.0 START at the parking lot, and head downhill toward the intersection. Cross Gambrill Park Road at this intersection and turn right. The trail runs parallel to the road beneath the power lines.

0.4 Reach the main trailhead parking lot at the bottom of the descent. Take a right, crossing the road and follow the yellow blazes.

0.6 Turn right at the trail intersection. Continue to follow the yellow blazes and get ready for a grinding steep uphill.

0.7 Continue left on the Yellow Trail at the storm shack. You are half way up the hill.

0.8 Turn left at the intersection. Continue following the yellow blazes.

0.9 Take a minute to soak in the view from the overlook. On a clear day looking south, you can see Crampton's Gap, a Civil War Landmark.

1.3 Reach the intersection of the Yellow and Black Trails. Continue straight. If you turn right, you will reach your starting point.

1.5 Make a sharp right. To your left are the Frederick Valley and a monumental view.

1.7 Continue straight following the Yellow Trail up the ascent. Get ready for the "Rock Garden," a truly technical section.

2.9 Finish the "Rock Garden." Did you dab? Continue following the yellow blazes.

(continues on next page)

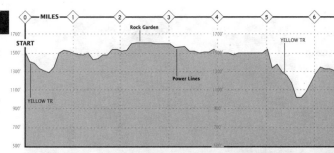

MilesDirections *(continued)*

3.1 Cross the road and follow the doubletrack into the woods.

3.3 Turn right at the power lines and head down the hill. Be careful. This is a fast and tricky descent.

3.5 Turn right at the end of the descent.

3.6 Continue following the Yellow Trail up the hill. Good luck.

4.0 Reach the gravel road and cross it. Continue straight on the Yellow Trail. At the doubletrack, bear left and continue downhill on the Yellow Trail.

4.2 Turn right into the woods. The trail is now blazed yellow and blue.

4.5 Turn left, heading downhill, bearing to the right. This will turn into an off-camber descent. Pay attention. This is a great descent.

4.8 Cross through this intersection and continue straight.

(continues on next page)

ficult. Remember, keep momentum on your side. The trail levels out for a while and ends at Gambrill Park Road with a short, fast descent. Cross the road onto the doubletrack and follow it to the power lines. Turn right here. This decent is fast and furious—you must pay attention to every nuance of the trail. A mistake here can cost you dearly.

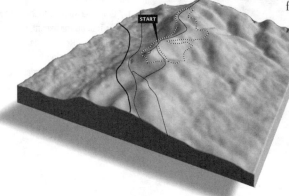

At the base, turn right, then immediately left, continuing to follow the yellow blazes. Shortly thereafter, the Yellow Trail continues to the

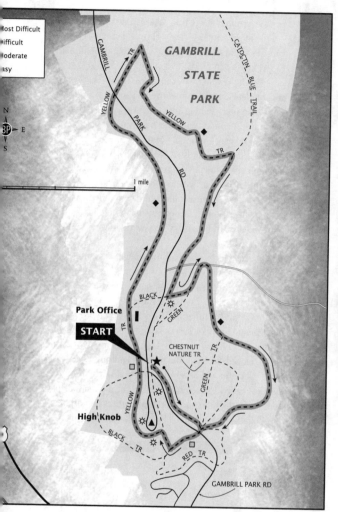

GAMBRILL STATE PARK

Most Difficult
Difficult
Moderate
Easy

N
BP — E
S

1 mile

GAMBRILL
PARK
RD

YELLOW
TR

CATOCTIN — BLUE — TRAIL

YELLOW
TR

BLACK

GREEN

Park Office
START

CHESTNUT
NATURE TR

GREEN
TR

High Knob

YELLOW
TR

BLACK — TR

RED — TR

GAMBRILL PARK RD

Ride Information

Trail Maintenance Hotline:
South Mountain Recreation Area
(301) 791-4767
TDD (301) 974 3683

Cost:
Only to use the picnic shelters, Tea Room, and campsites

Schedule:
Open daily from dawn to dusk

Maps:
USGS maps: Myersville, MD;
    Catoctin Furnace, MD;
    Middletown, MD; Frederick, MD
ADC Maps: Frederick, MD road map
    Gambrill State Park trail map
DeLorme: Maryland/Delaware Atlas
    & Gazetteer – Page 72 D-2

Miles Directions (continued)

5.2 What a descent! Turn right. It's time to pay your dues and head straight up the hill along the Yellow Trail, continuing straight through the next two intersections.
5.8 Back at the parking lot. Turn right and continue on the Yellow Trail up the first descent. If you'd like, choose another loop from the trail map.
6.3 Back at the intersection. Turn left toward High Knob and your car. What a ride!

right back up the mountain and meanders through the forest. You will reach a short descent along a fire road and turn right heading back into the forest. The trail is now blazed yellow and blue. From here, the trail follows a long, off-camber descent that will test all your riding skills. Once at the bottom, take a minute to catch your breath. Loosen up and prepare yourself for the tough climb back to the parking lot. Once at the lot, take a right and continue up toward the High Knob Scenic Area. This should be a ride that you will not soon forget.

Catoctin Blue Trail

Start: Trailhead parking lot: Gambrill State Park
Length: 10.5 miles
Rating: Very Difficult due to the severity of blue trail's terrain, steep climbs, and mileage
Terrain: Rugged singletrack, paved and dirt roads

Getting There

From **Frederick, MD** – Take **Route-40 west** (Baltimore National Pike) and turn **right** on **Shookstown Road.** Follow Shookstown Road to **Gambrill Park Road** and turn **right.** Go 0.5 miles up Gambrill Park Road and park in the small parking lot on the right side of the road just before the hill gets very steep.

The terrain is steep, the rocks are hard, and the trail is mostly unforgiving. This is perhaps one of Maryland's toughest trails open to mountain bike riding.

The Catoctin Trail leads you deep into Gambrill and Frederick State Forest over relentless singletrack that will have your body aching for pavement—that is unless you've loaded the suspension onto your bike. For those skeptics of bicycle suspension, here's your chance to test its mettle.

On the lighter side, tall stands of chestnut oak, hickory, and black birch canopy the Catoctin Mountain, shielding out hints of a more hectic world beyond its wooded boundaries. Only refreshing sounds of cascading streams, calling birds, and the footsteps of local deer are heard—and the occasional sound of bicycle chains slapping against frames as cyclists warily negotiate their way down the rugged trails.

The Catoctin Trail starts where all trails begin in Gambrill— from the parking lot on the east side of Gambrill Park Road. In its entirety, the Catoctin Trail travels north nearly 18 miles through Gambrill State Park, Frederick Watershed, Cunningham Falls State Park, and Catoctin Mountain National Park. Unfortunately, mountain bike access is cut short just north of Frederick Watershed. Follow the dark blue blazes up and down Catoctin's steep, jagged slopes all the way to Hamburg Road.

The name "Catoctin" is believed to come from a tribe of Native Americans called Kittoctons who lived at the foothills of the mountains along the Potomac. European settlers first arrived in 1732 from Philadelphia, attracted by Lord Baltimore's offer of

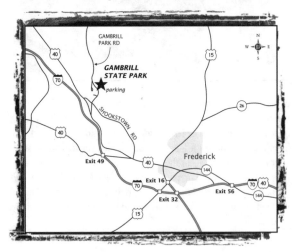

MilesDirections

0.0 START at the trailhead parking lot, where all the trails begin. Follow the Blue Trail into the forest, heading north. This quickly becomes a steep, rocky, fast descent straight down the mountain.

0.6 Come to a trail intersection. Turn right, following the Blue Trail (indicated by the blue blazes on the trees).

0.7 Bear left up the mountain, continuing on the Blue/Yellow trail.

1.4 Reach the summit of this brutally steep climb. Blue/Yellow Trail splits. Turn left off the present trail, then immediately right, continuing on the blue trail. The Yellow Trail goes left at this point and heads back toward High Knob.

1.6 Turn right on the dirt road (you will turn off this road very soon).

1.65 Turn left off the dirt road back into the woods, continuing on the blue trail. (Keep your eyes peeled to the left for the blue blazes on the trees. This trailhead is difficult to spot). Begin a very long, steep, rocky descent down the mountain.

2.8 Reach the bottom of the long, rocky descent. It's beautiful down here! Turn left, crossing the stream, and continue on the Blue Trail. Start climbing again up this mountainside. This climb is even more brutal!

(continues on next page)

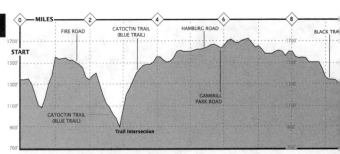

MilesDirections*(continued)*

3.6 Reach the summit. Finally! How does the back feel?

5.5 Turn left on Hamburg Road (dirt road).

5.9 Turn right on Gambrill Park Road (paved).

9.3 Turn right off Gambrill Park Road on the Black Trail. This turn-off is just before the first stone overlook to the left. (You should see the black arrow pointing the way).

9.4 Turn left on the Yellow/Black trail.

9.6 Bear left, continuing down. Overlook on the right.

9.8 Turn right at the turn near the main road, continuing to follow the Black Trail.

10.5 Cross Gambrill Park Road and arrive at the trailhead parking lot. You deserve a serious drink after that ride!

200 acres of rent-free land for three years. The land would then cost only one cent per acre per year. Much of the land used by these early settlers was for logging and for supplying charcoal to local iron furnaces. Catoctin's resources, though, were eventually stripped and depleted from extensive clear-cutting. Then, in 1935, the federal government purchased more than 10,000 acres of this land to be made into a recreational area. The National Park Service and Maryland Park Service manage the land today, permitting Catoctin to redevelop back into the hardwood forest of pre-European settlement.

This trail is not recommended to the novice off-road cyclist and should be considered extremely challenging to those well-versed in rugged terrain.

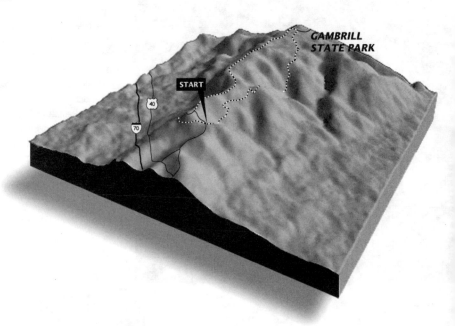

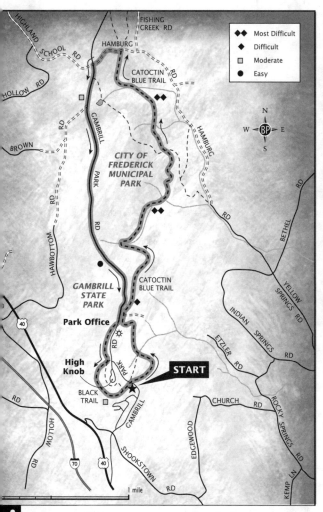

Most Difficult ◆◆
Difficult ◆
Moderate □
Easy ●

HIGHLAND
HIGHLAND SCHOOL RD
HOLLOW RD
FISHING CREEK RD
HAMBURG
CATOCTIN BLUE TRAIL
BROWN RD
GAMBRILL PARK RD
CITY OF FREDERICK MUNICIPAL PARK
HAMBURG RD
BETHEL RD
N W E S BP
RD
HAWBOTTOM RD
CATOCTIN BLUE TRAIL
YELLOW SPRINGS RD
INDIAN SPRINGS RD
GAMBRILL STATE PARK
Park Office
40
High Knob
START
ETZLER RD
RD
BLACK TRAIL
CHURCH RD
ROCKY SPRINGS RD
RD
HOLLOW RD
EDGEWOOD
GAMBRILL
SHOOKSTOWN RD
KEMP LN
70 40
1 mile

Ride Information

Trail Maintenance Hotline:
South Mountain Recreation Area
(301) 791-4767
TDD (301) 974 3683

Cost:
Only to use the picnic shelters, Tea Room, and campsites

Schedule:
Open daily from dawn to dusk

Maps:
USGS maps: Myersville, MD;
Catoctin Furnace, MD;
Middletown, MD; Frederick, MD
ADC Maps: Frederick, MD road
map
DeLorme: Maryland/Delaware Atlas
& Gazetteer – Page 72 D-2
Gambrill State Park trail map

In Addition...

We hear all the time that our president has lifted off from the White House and gone on retreat to Camp David. But did you know that Camp David is located just a few miles north of here in Catoctin Mountain Park? This 134-acre presidential retreat was established in 1942 by Franklin Roosevelt, who named it Shangri-La. President Eisenhower renamed the hideaway to Camp David in 1953 after his grandson. The most famous summit conference held at Camp David was what is today called the Camp David Accord, which took place in September 1979 between Egypt's President Anwar Sadat and Israel's Prime Minister Menachem Begin. President Carter hosted the accord and provided what all parties now call a "framework for peace" in the Middle East.

Sugarloaf's Scenic Circuit

Ride Specs

Start: Sugarloaf Park entrance in Stronghold
Length: 12 miles
Rating: Moderate
Terrain: Paved/unpaved roads
Other Uses: Horseback, automobiles

Getting There

From the **Capital Beltway (495)** – Take **I-270 north** approximately 21 miles to the **Hyattstown exit (Exit 22)**. Circle under I-270, heading **southwest** on **Route 109 (Old Hundred Road)**. Follow Old Hundred Road three miles to Comus, then turn **right** on **Comus Road**. You will see Sugarloaf Mountain from here. Follow Comus Road straight into **Stronghold** to the entrance of the mountain. There is parking, but it is extremely tight. So **get here early.**

From the **Baltimore Beltway (695)** – Take **I-70 west** approximately 38 miles to **Frederick, MD.** From Frederick, follow **I-270 south** 9.5 miles to the **Hyattstown exit (Exit 22)**. Get on **Route 109 (Old Hundred Road)** and continue as above.

Named after the sugar loaf by early pioneers because of its shape, Sugarloaf Mountain stands at an elevation of 1,282 feet, more than 800 feet above the Monocacy Valley. The mountain dominates the landscape for miles in all directions and has attracted its share of attention throughout history. The earliest known map of Sugarloaf was sketched by a Swiss explorer in 1707 while the United States was still part of the colonies of Britain. It is noted that General Braddock marched past the mountain in 1775 during the French and Indian War. Later in American history during the Civil War the mountain was a matter of contention between the North and South as its summit and overlooks provided ideal observation of the valleys below.

During the very early part of the twentieth century the mountain's main peak and surrounding land was purchased by Gordon Strong who, in 1946, organized Stronghold, Incorporated, a non-profit organization designed for "enjoyment and education in an appreciation of natural beauty." Strong's original intent was for a vacation retreat. He built the Strong Mansion atop the mountain and a number of homes at the foot of the mountain in what is now Stronghold. Since Strong's death in 1954, Stronghold, Inc. has continued to manage the 3,250 acres of land on and around Sugarloaf Mountain as a place of natural beauty and wildlife, committed to maintaining its natural state.

This loop travels on both paved and unpaved roads surrounding Sugarloaf Mountain, which is always looming above you as you pedal past magnificent horse farms and along the rushing waters of Bennett Creek. This is not a ride recommended

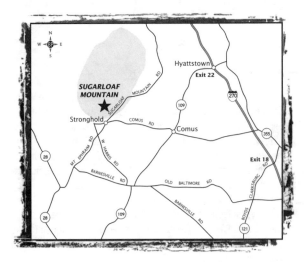

MilesDirections

0.0 START from the park entrance at the base of the mountain in Stronghold. Facing east, turn left on Sugarloaf Mountain Road. This road starts out paved, then turns to gravel after a quarter mile.

2.5 Turn left on Thurston Road (paved).

4.8 Turn hard left on Peters Road (becomes unpaved).

7.0 Turn left on Park Mills Road (paved).

7.7 Turn left on Mount Ephraim Road (unpaved).

11.5 Turn left on Comus Road (unpaved).

11.9 Arrive back at Stronghold. What a gorgeous ride!

for a regular road bike, since many roads are gravel and dirt. As you climb back over the mountain toward Stronghold on Mount Ephraim Road, all remnants of pavement disappear and you are transported deep into a mountain forest.

Geologically speaking, Sugarloaf Mountain is what's called a monadnock. This is a hill or mountain that remains standing high above the surface after much of the surrounding land has eroded away. It took nearly 14 million years for Sugarloaf to look like it does today.

This is a great ride for cyclists wanting the adventure and unique scenery often associated with riding off the beaten path, but not interested in the severe challenges of singletrack trails twisting up and down the mountain slopes.

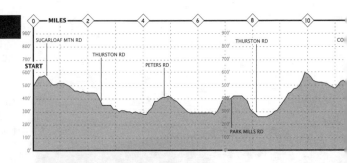

In Addition...

Back in 1993, under the staff supervision of the Stronghold Corporation, groups of off-road cyclists, hikers, and Boy Scouts worked together to create a trail system that combined both forest roads and challenging singletrack on which to ride. The result was a fantastic course ideal for mountain biking, hiking, and horseback riding. Unfortunately, the trail's popularity was far more than its narrow, twisting pathways could bear, as hundreds of cyclists each weekend saddled up and crowded its course. Land managers were forced to reassess the trail's design and concluded that, with parking spilling into nearby towns and the trail's capacity heavily overextended, limited access was the only answer. Currently, the Saddleback Trail is open to cyclists only on weekdays. While this may appear unfair and inconvenient to some, remember that Sugarloaf Mountain is a privately owned resource. Thankfully, the Stronghold Corporation is generous enough to allow the Saddleback Trail to remain open to cyclists at all.

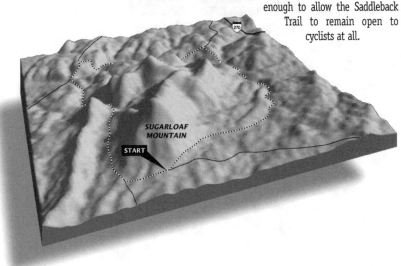

Ride Information

Trail Maintenance Hotline:
Stronghold Corporation
(301) 869-7846
Sugarloaf Mountain Staff
(301) 874-2024

Schedule:
Sugarloaf Mountain Park and
Stronghold Corporation open daily
from early morning to sunset, year-
round

Maps:
USGS maps: Buckeystown, MD;
  Urbana, MD
ADC Maps: Frederick road map
DeLorme: Maryland/Delaware Atlas
  & Gazetteer – Page 55 C-6

River Ride

Ride Specs

Start: Whites Ferry
Length: 10 miles
Rating: Easy
Terrain: Hard dirt (towpath); unpaved roads
Other Uses: Hiking, horseback riding, automobiles

Getting There

Maryland – From the **Capital Beltway** – Take **I-270 North** and go 10.5 miles to **MD-117 west**. Turn **left** at the second stoplight on **MD-124 (Quince Orchard Road)**. Go 2.8 miles on Quince Orchard Road, and then make a **right** at the stoplight on **MD-28 (Darnestown Road)**. Bear left after 6 miles on **MD-107 (Fisher Ave then Whites Ferry Road)**. Continue for 11.3 miles to **Whites Ferry on the Potomac** and park in the parking lot on the right.

Northern Virginia – From the **Capital Beltway** – Take **Exit 10, Route 7 west (Leesburg Pike)** all the way to Leesburg (22 miles). Just before Leesburg, take **Route 15 (James Monroe Highway) north**. Go approximately 3.5 miles on Route 15, and then make a **right** turn on **Whites Ferry Road**. This will take you down to the ferry. You must pay the **$2.00 toll** and cross the river to park and begin the ride.

This easygoing loop along the Potomac River connects two places that, at one time, signified an age when the ferry was the most convenient means across the river. The ride begins at Whites Ferry and travels south along flat dirt roads to Edwards Ferry, which quit operations in 1936.

At one point, during the 1700s, there were at least seven ferries carrying Loudoun county residents across the Potomac. Records of the county court show that by the end of the eighteenth century, not long after the signing of our Declaration of Independence, five ferries crossed the Potomac to connect the Maryland and Virginia shores, one of which was Edwards. Whites Ferry, formerly known as Conrad's Ferry, began operations in 1836, carrying horse-drawn wagons, merchants, and supplies from shore to shore. Later in the nineteenth century, Whites and Edwards Ferries served quite different purposes, however, and the results were often disastrous.

During the Civil War, both Union and Confederate troops used the ferries to carry troops back and forth across the Potomac. In one instance, on the night of October 20, 1861, Union troops under General Stone's command at Edwards Ferry and Whites Ferry reported a Confederate camp near Leesburg. In an attempt to intimidate the Confederates to leave the area, General Stone set in motion events that ultimately resulted in the Battle of Ball's Bluff (see page 106), costing the Union a severe and gruesome loss. Alternately, Confederate General Jubal A. Early, for whom the present ferryboat at Whites Ferry is named,

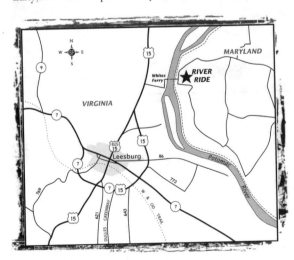

MilesDirections

0.0 START at the Whites Ferry parking lot on the Maryland side of the Potomac River. Approximately 50 feet north of the parking lot, turn right off Whites Ferry Road on River Road (unpaved). This runs parallel to the C&O canal towpath to the right.

3.7 At the three-way intersection, continue right on River Road.

5.2 Turn right on Edwards Ferry Road. Cross over the C&O Canal and arrive at Edwards Ferry. Return along the C&O towpath back to Whites Ferry.

10.0 Arrive at Whites Ferry parking lot.

used both Edwards Ferry and Whites Ferry in retreat after his daring attack on Washington in July 1864.

Today, Whites Ferry is the last of the ferries to carry customers across the Potomac, operating seven days a week from 6:00 a.m. to 11:00 p.m. In fact, it's the only place between Point of Rocks, Maryland, and the Capital Beltway, to cross the river—a stretch of 40 miles.

As you ride back along the C&O Canal towpath, be sure to notice Harrison Island on your left. During the Civil War, the island served as a temporary hospital to care for the Union's wounded soldiers after their dramatic loss at the battle on Ball's Bluff. One of the wounded taken to Harrison Island was recent Harvard graduate and future Supreme Court Justice, First Lieutenant Oliver Wendell Holmes, Jr. He was shot through the leg and the small of the back, but was diagnosed on the island as "doing well."

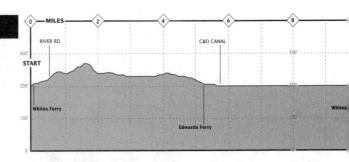

This ride, rich in history, is meant for the lighter side of mountain biking, as it travels along flat dirt roads and the C&O Canal towpath. You won't have to worry much about traffic, and should enjoy pedaling past an enormous replica of what many homeowners work a lifetime to achieve—a perfect lawn. The Summit Hall Turf Farm, along River Road, grows a magnificent 380-acre "lawn," carpeted in thick green zoysia, blue grass, bent grass, and mixtures of blue and rye grass. The sod is then harvested and sent to area golf courses, local landscapers, and some very fortunate homeowners.

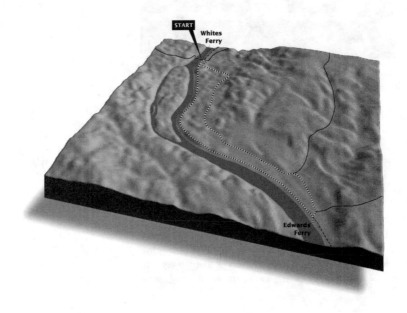

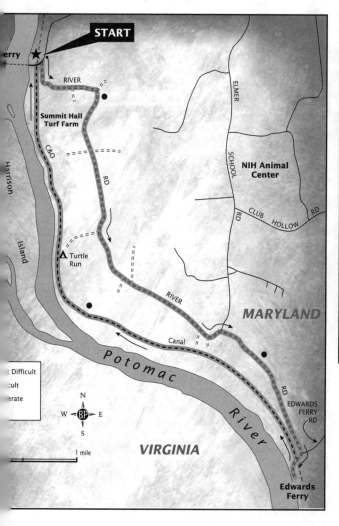

START

Ride Information

Trail Maintenance Hotline:
C&O Canal Headquarters: (301)
739-4200
Summit Hall Turf Farm: (301) 948-
2900

Costs:
The ferry is $2 per car, 50¢ per
bicycle

Maps:
USGS maps: Waterford, VA, MD;
   Poolesville, VA, MD; Leesburg,
   VA, MD; Sterling, VA, MD
ADC Maps: Montgomery County,
   MD
DeLorme: Maryland/Delaware Atlas
   & Gazetteer – Page 55 D-4

Black Hill State Park

Ride Specs

Start: Little Seneca Lake, parking lot #5
Length: 9.0 miles
Rating: Easy to Moderate
Terrain: Mostly singletrack – 0.6 miles of asphalt trail – 0.5 miles of paved road
Other Uses: Hiking, fitness course, boating, fishing, horseback riding

Getting There

From **Washington** – Take **I-270 north** and exit on **Route 118 East.** Approximately one-half mile on Route 118 turn **left on Route 355 north.** Follow Route 355 north and turn **left on West Old Baltimore Road.** Follow this road for 1.5 miles to the park entrance and turn **left on Lake Ridge Drive.** Follow Lake Ridge Drive to **parking lot #5** close to the restrooms (far end) overlooking **Little Seneca Lake.**

Montgomery County, the most populated county in Maryland, was established by State Convention in 1776 and functioned under the County Commission System until 1948. Since then, voters adopted a charter giving the county home-rule with a council manager form of government. Named for Revolutionary War General Richard Montgomery, the county is as diverse as its parks and people.

Black Hill Regional Park, a popular area for all sorts of recreation, is situated in the northern part of Montgomery County, near Gaithersburg and Germantown. Black Hill is home to mountain biking, hiking, horseback riding, boating, fishing, and more.

Upon entering the park, visitors are treated to an outstanding view of Little Seneca Lake. The lake was built through the partnership of the Maryland National Park and Planning Commission and the Washington Suburban Sanitary Commission. Its design marked it as a dual-purpose lake both for recreation as well as an emergency water supply for the Washington Metropolitan area. After a ride, consider having a picnic on the shores overlooking the lake or perhaps renting a boat and going for a sail ($4.75 per hour for rowboat & canoe, $2.00 per person for pontoon boat rides).

In the summertime, expect the lake to be full of activity such as sailboats, canoes, and fishermen. In the fall, if you're here at the right time (early to mid-October), you may be treated to some of the area's most impressive fall colors. When you're ready to leave, take a short trip to Germantown and Olde Town Gaithersburg, two of Maryland's most prosperous little cities.

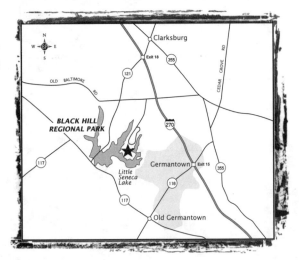

Unlike many areas of Maryland, the Germantown/ Gaithersburg area doesn't show much evidence of early Indian settlements. However, its proximity to the Potomac and Monocacy Rivers as well as Seneca Creek made this area a very popular location for Native American living. It is believed that after the annual spring floods, Indians from the Piscataway, Susquehannock, and Seneca tribes traveled to this area to hunt the roaming herds of bison and other large animals trapped by the swollen waters. Many of the trails by which the Native Americans traveled to reach this hunting ground later became the same routes and roadways that we use today, including Clopper Road, Route 28, Route 118, and Route 355.

In the early to mid-1800s, several German immigrants, most of whom were from German settlements in Pennsylvania, moved down to this area of Maryland and set up livelihoods along the intersections of Clopper Road and the Darnestown/Neelsville Road (Route 118). This settlement quickly became known as Germantown.

At about the same time, just south of Germantown, many of the younger sons of Maryland's Chesapeake Bay settlers began establishing themselves in the vast, fertile land of Montgomery County. One of the earliest settlements in this area—dating back to 1802—was known as Forest Oak, named for the landmark tree still standing near the railroad crossing on Frederick Avenue. Today this area is called Gaithersburg. In 1802, a young settler to

MilesDirections

0.0 START at parking lot #5. Ride away from the lake toward the restrooms, following the hiker/biker sign to the paved trail.

0.3 Turn right on the paved trail at the Par-course Fitness Circuit sign.

0.7 Turn right on the unpaved trail immediately after the ring station of the Par-course Fitness Section.

1.0 Continue straight at this small trail intersection. At this point you should be traveling parallel to Lake Ridge Drive.

1.5 Reach the intersection with the forest service road. Continue straight. If you turn right, you will head toward the Waters Landing Housing Community.

1.6 Turn left at this intersection and head uphill.

1.7 Cross the underground gas lines and continue straight.

1.9 At this trail intersection bear right. This trail is blazed with blue diamonds and white letters. Make a wide U-turn and head uphill. You are now riding in the opposite direction, parallel to the previous trail.

2.3 Cross the forest service road and continue straight on "Hard Rock Trail." Reach a field immediately after this intersection. Continue straight.

2.5 Turn right into the woods at the "Hard Rock Trail" pylon.

2.7 You can hear traffic on I-270. Bear right at this intersection and continue toward I-270. A fun twisty singletrack descent awaits.

(continues on next page)

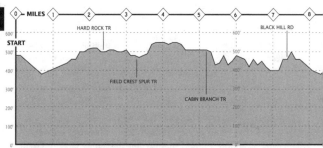

MilesDirections (continued)

2.9 Cross the creek and continue paralleling I-270.

3.3 Reach the intersection of I-270 and West Old Baltimore Road. Turn left on West Old Baltimore Road and head up the hill for approximately one tenth of a mile. Look for the Field Crest Spur trailhead on your left.

3.6 Bear right and follow the doubletrack to the right.

3.7 Turn left and head back toward Hard Rock Trail.

3.8 Turn right on the singletrack into the woods.

4.3 Turn right at this intersection. If you wish, turn left and do the 1.5-mile loop (starting from Marker 2.7) all over again.

4.5 Reach the field again. Continue straight through the grass.

4.6 Turn left at the Hill Crest pylon and continue riding through the grass.

4.7 Turn left into the woods (not the grass trail) along the double-track. This trail is blazed blue with white letters.

4.8 Turn right and head up this trail that you were on earlier in the ride.

5.2 Turn right and cross Lake Ridge Drive. Follow the trailhead marked "Cabin Branch Trail" on the other side of the road. Get ready for a great descent. Continue straight on this trail.

5.9 Turn left on the AT&T right-of-way (marked with orange pylons).

(continues on next page)

the area named Benjamin Gaither built his house on this fertile land unknowingly giving his name to the town.

With the arrival of the railroad and the invention of the automobile, businesses in Germantown and Gaithersburg began to prosper. Farmers planted and harvested more crops, easily transporting them to other markets throughout the area. Farmers no longer had to make several trips to town. With a newly built steam mill, they could make a single trip to mill their grains, purchase supplies, and market their products all from the railroad. The railroad also brought people in from Washington. Soon it became fashionable to escape to the "country" and many large estates were built.

Today, Germantown and Gaithersburg are prosperous and growing communities with combined populations reaching nearly one million. In the last couple of decades, both Gaithersburg and Germantown have seen a major boom in development. Its proximity to Washington, DC, and Frederick, Maryland, have made this part of Montgomery County an attractive business location as well as residential getaway. As you travel to Black Hill Regional Park, you can't help but witness the amount of

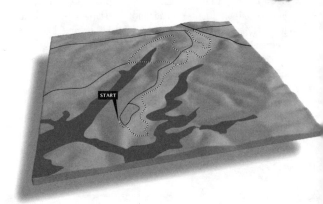

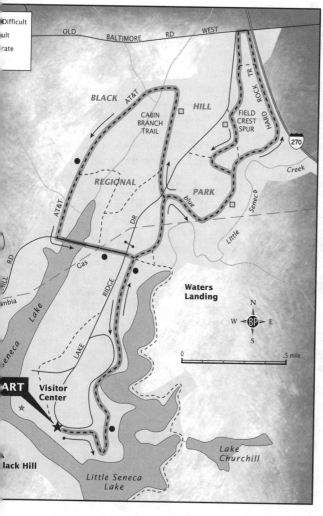

Ride Information

Trail Maintenance Hotline:
Black Hill Regional Park Office
Jim McMahon
20930 Lake Ridge Drive
Boyds, MD 20841
(301) 972-9396

Schedule
March 1 – October 31
6 a.m. to sunset
November 1 – February 28
7 a.m. to sunset
Park Closed:
Thanksgiving
Christmas and New Year's

Maps:
USGS maps: Germantown, MD
ADC Maps: Montgomery County,
MD
DeLorme: Maryland/Delaware Atlas
& Gazetteer – Page 56 D-1

MilesDirections(continued)

6.7 Continue straight, heading up the AT&T right-of-way. In the summer time, this trail is flanked on both sides with colorful wildflowers.

6.9 View of Little Seneca Lake.

7.1 Turn left on Black Hill Road.

7.4 Cross Lake Ridge Drive, then head straight through the yellow gate into the woods along the forest service road.

7.5 Turn right at this intersection. You should now be back on the trail you first started on.

8.5 Turn left on the paved trail.

8.8 Turn left at the paved trail intersection.

9.0 Reach the parking lot.

new development still going on along I-270's "Technology Corridor." You will be pleasantly surprised to find Black Hill Regional Park (among others) an oasis in the middle of this massive development. Although the lake did not exist when the first settlers came to the area, the beauty, abundance of wildlife, and thick forests in the park give you a glimpse and a sampling of this area's historic past.

Schaeffer Farms

1

Ride Specs

Length: 3.7 miles
Start: Staging Area
Rating: Easy to Moderate
Terrain: Singletrack
Other Uses: Equestrian, hiking

Getting There

From **Washington** – Take I-270 north to **Route 117 west (Clopper Road).** Go approximately 4.5 miles along Clopper Road. Just past the 8th light at Route 118 (Darnestown-Germantown Road) turn **left on Schaeffer Road.** Follow Schaeffer Road for 2.0 miles then turn **left at Black Burn Farm.** Follow the "Trails Parking" sign to the trailhead.

O nce again, the efforts of a few individuals pay off for everyone. MORE members Dave McGill and Dave Skull achieved what few have been able to do in Montgomery County, Maryland, since mountain biking became popular—blaze and build new, legal mountain bike trails. Thanks to their efforts and those of many other active mountain bikers, a steady series of new trails have been built in and adjacent to Seneca Creek State Park.

Schaeffer Farms, near Germantown (northern Montgomery County), is within the boundaries of Seneca Creek State Park. This area is part of a stream valley that extends approximately 12 miles along Seneca Creek. These new trails are located primarily on a portion of land leased by the county to local farmers who use it to grow corn and a variety of other vegetables.

For some time, an adjacent tract of nearly 2,000 acres lay undeveloped and overgrown. Today, a four-mile loop is completed with approximately six more miles under way. When all is said and done, Schaeffer Farms will have up to 10 miles of new singletrack for cyclists to enjoy. MORE's trail construction and maintenance efforts in this park and within Fountainhead Regional Park *(see ride #30 on page 138)* earned them IMBA's 1996 Model Program Award.

Park officials initially wanted the trails to be exclusive to mountain bikes, but were persuaded by trail organizers to keep the area open to everyone, making it a multi-use trail system. Equestrians, hikers, and mountain bikers alike are welcome and find it perfect for whatever their activity is.

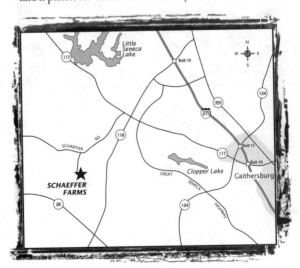

MilesDirections

Loop A

0.0 START from the parking area and enter at the trailhead marked by IMBA's "Share The Trail" sign.

0.25 Bear left at this trail intersection (the right fork dead ends less than a mile ahead).

0.97 Reach the bottom of the hill at the hollow stump. Follow the brown trail marker with white blazes to your right.

1.08 After a series of three small creak crossings bear left into the woods and continue along the trail parallel to the gas lines.

1.3 Bear left into the woods, continuing to follow the white blazes.

2.3 Cross the forest service road, continuing straight into the grove of pines.

2.4 Turn right at the cornfields (respect the stalks, this is private property). After a short climb get ready for some fun descents.

2.6 Bear right into the woods, then head back to the left. The cornfield should now be on your right

2.8 Reach a series of small switchbacks. Watch out for the drop-off at the bottom. Continue, following the white blazes.

3.7 Reach an opening. Turn right and arrive back at the parking area. Now try it in the opposite direction.

(continues on next page)

MilesDirections(continued)

MILES · 0 · 1 · 2 · 3 · 4 · 5 · 6 · 7

500' — — 500'

START

400' — — 400'

END

LOOP 'A'   LOOP 'B'

Loop B

"Loop B" covers a much larger area but is similar to "Loop A" in terrain. By combining both of these loops into one ride, you can cover as many as 11 miles. "Loop B" is clearly marked with yellow blazes.

0.0 START from the parking area and enter at the trailhead marked by IMBA's "Share The Trail" sign.
0.25 Bear right at the trail intersection (the left fork takes you to "Loop A").
0.37 Come out of the woods into the fields. The trail continues to the left.
0.40 Head back into the woods along singletrack.
0.93 Come out into the field again. This section skirts the treeline to the left. The trail is marked with flagged stakes.
1.07 Turn into the woods along singletrack. The trail is clearly blazed yellow.
3.07 Wow! The last two miles were great. Continue following the yellow blazes.
3.44 Continue straight through this intersection. On your way back, you will come from the left and double back the last three miles.
3.64 Continue to the left. (The right fork will take you to "Loop C"— under construction at the time of this first printing.)
3.75 After crossing the creek, the trail continues to the right, up and to the left.

(continues on next page)

Your ride begins adjacent to the Black Burn Farm in the Trail Staging Area. The trail is clearly marked with a brown pylon and an IBMA (International Mountain Biking Association) trail etiquette sign. Continue straight on some tight singletrack then bear left at the first intersection. To the right is the second loop within this park. Continue through the next section—a twisting up and down roller coaster-like trail filled with surprises. It becomes obvious once you're on this trail that it was built by mountain bikers and not park officials.

After a series of small creek crossings, you will begin the first of a handful of climbs. A quarter of a mile later, turn left into the woods onto the singletrack. Follow the white blazes for approximately one mile. At mile marker 2.3, cross the fire road and enter into the woods and through the grove of pines.

Shortly after, turn right and ride adjacent to the cornfield. If you manage to hit the trail at the right time of year when the corn is high and the vegetation is thick, it may appear that you're in a corn stalk tunnel. Don't give in to temptation. Leave the corn alone.

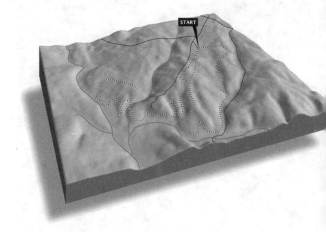

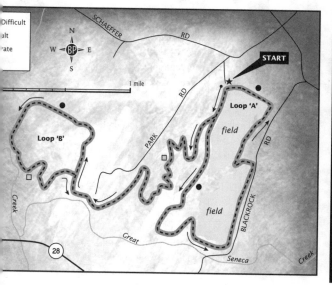

Ride Information

Trail Maintenance Hotline:
MORE (703) 502-0359
more@cycling.org

Schedule:
Open daily, from dawn til dusk

Maps:
USGS maps: Germantown, MD
ADC Maps: Montgomery County,
    MD
DeLorme: Maryland/Delaware Atlas
    & Gazetteer – Page 56 D-1

There is plenty of sweet corn at the local vegetable stands.

Continue down through a series of switchbacks (be careful, yours truly biffed at the bottom of the last switchback right into the creek). After crossing the creek, turn left and continue following the white blazes. The last half-mile is on a flat twisty section of single-track full of fun log jumps and bunny hops. 3.7 miles later you're back where you parked. Now turn around and do the whole ride in the opposite direction. You know what they say; "It's a whole new trail in the opposite direction." This trail has all the makings to be a classic mountain bike route. Its curves and whoop-de-doos make it a lot of fun. What it lacks in length is easily made up in challenging terrain. If you're interested in helping to build new trails like this one, contact your local mountain bike club and get involved.

MilesDirections(continued)

4.05 After a small gully, turn left and follow the treeline.
4.25 Continue to the right.
4.4 Turn right and follow the tree-line.
4.65 Follow the trail into the trees.
4.75 Turn right at this intersection and head toward the creek.
4.8 After crossing the creek, turn right and follow the treeline.
5.0 Turn left on the doubletrack trail. There is a small sign on the ground pointing in the direction from which you just came.
5.20 Turn right into the woods onto the singletrack trail and backtrack to the start of the ride.
8.7 Reach the parking lot where you began.

Seneca Creek State Park

H ere's a short but challenging ride around Seneca Creek State Park's Clopper Lake, taking you along tricky singletrack trails, through undeveloped natural areas, across open fields, along the lake's shores, and past evidence of times long past.

You'll begin the ride following the Lake Shore Trail, which crosses old fields and skirts the lake's shoreline. In the spring and summer these fields are filled with colorful wildflowers that give way in the fall to thick, golden sagegrass. Just before the dam you'll be treated to a spectacular view of the lake from King Fisher Overlook. The trail quickly descends across the park road and follows Long Draught Branch, winding up, down, and around beneath a dense canopy of gray birch before crossing the wooded boardwalk to Mink Hollow Trail. Seneca Creek's longest developed trail, Mink Hollow, travels through pine groves and habitats of local wildlife, including white tail deer. Be careful, once you begin the challenging ride along the undeveloped trail edging around the lake. This trail can be tricky and challenging as exposed roots, steep inclines, occasional flooding, and some quick descents may trip you up if you're not focused.

While Seneca Creek Park extends nearly 13 miles from Gaithersburg south to the Potomac, only this northern section around Clopper Lake is developed for recreation. The lake itself is relatively new, created by damming Long Draught Branch. However, the name "Clopper" has a rich history in this area, dating back to the early 1800s when Francis C. Clopper, a successful tobacco merchant from Philadelphia, purchased more than

Ride Specs

Start: Clopper Lake boat center
Length: 5 miles
Rating: Easy to Moderate
Terrain: Singletrack trails
Other Uses: Hiking, boating, fishing, horseback riding, picnicking

Getting There

From the **Capital Beltway (495)** – Take **I-270 north** toward Frederick. Just after passing through Gaithersburg on I-270 take the exit for **Route 124 west (Orchard Road)** to Darnesville. Follow Route 124 west 1/2 mile, then turn **right on Route 117 (Clopper Road).** Go 1.5 miles on Clopper Road to the entrance to **Seneca Creek State Park** on the left. Follow the entrance road into the park. You may park at any of the lots available, including the visitors center—first stop on the right. You may also park at the boat center, but driving the car through the main gate may cost you a couple of dollars as an entrance fee.

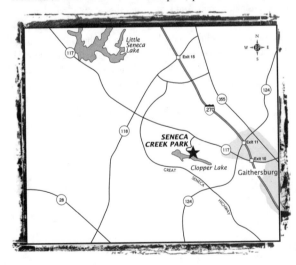

540 acres and an existing mill on Seneca Creek. The mill's most prosperous years were between 1830 and 1880, during which time Francis Clopper farmed the land and raised his family. The land remained in the hands of four generations of Clopper's descendants until 1955 when the state purchased it and added the land to Seneca Creek State Park.

Throughout the park there is evidence of this past; abandoned farms and old meadows now covered by new growth, traces of many of Clopper's old mills, and many of Clopper's old farm

lanes. Mill ruins can still be seen from the intersection of Clopper Road and Waring Station Road, just west of the park entrance, and traces of the Clopper home are evident nearby the visitor center.

Please be aware, as always, that many other outdoor enthusiasts share these same trails. Always yield the right of way to any other trail users, and ride cautiously, as the trails have many hidden turns and difficult negotiations.

MilesDirections

0.0 START at Clopper Lake's boat center (soda machines available). Ride west to the end of the circular drive and go straight into the grass on the other side. Follow Lake Shore Trail (blue) signs.

0.3 The Lake Shore Trail (blue) drops you into an open field. On the other side of this field you will notice the blue trailhead marker. Cross the field and continue on Lake Shore Trail. To the left is the dam.

0.5 Lake Shore Trail (blue) brings you right up to King Fisher Overlook. You can catch a nice view of the lake from here. Follow the remainder of the blue-blazed trail into the woods, which re-enters the woods at the back-side of the circular drive. Go down the little hill through the woods and immediately cross the road.

0.55 Long Draught Trail (yellow) begins catty corner to where the Blue Trail ends.

1.1 Turn left on Mink Hollow Trail (white).

1.2 Bear left, continuing on Mink Hollow Trail (white) over a narrow boardwalk, crossing the creek.

1.8 Cross the park road. Continue straight on the White Trail.

2.2 Mink Hollow Trail (white) comes to the lake. Turn right, following the trail around the lake.

(continues on next page)

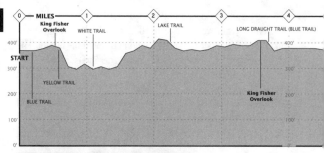

MilesDirections*(continued)*

3.4 This trail zips up on Long Draught Road. Cross Long Draught Road on the asphalt path. Once you're across the bridge, turn left through the guardrail and back on the trail around the lake.

3.7 This trail drops you down on a flat, gravel path. Turn right. Left takes you to a dead-end at the lake. Stay on this gravel path only about 20 feet. Then turn left across the creek to hook up with the path that continues to follow the perimeter of the lake.

4.3 Turn left, crossing over a little wooden bridge at the end of the alcove. Continue following the trail.

4.7 Arrive at the boat center and grab a soda from the soda machine. What a ride!

In Addition...

If you're interested in Maryland, facts and figures taken from the 1990 Census provide a little insight into what each of its largest cities and towns are all about.

Baltimore (pop. 736,014). Seaport on Patapsco River; historic and industrial city; automobile assembly; metals; chemicals; printing; clothing; shipping, insurance, and financial center; Fort McHenry; Washington Monument; Johns Hopkins University.

Rockville (pop. 44,835). Residential city; biomedical technology; computer science; telecommunications; grave of F. Scott Fitzgerald; Strathmore Hall Arts Center; Montgomery College.

Frederick (pop. 40,148). Industrial city in farm area; electronics and communications; biological products; air conditioning equipment; clothing; cancer research; Barbara Fritchie House and Museum; Hood College.

Gaithersburg (pop. 39,542). Suburb of Washington, DC; center for research and development; biomedical technology; computer science; telecommunications; Seneca Creek State Recreational Area nearby.

Bowie (pop. 37,589). Residential and cultural area; International Renaissance Center; University of Maryland Science and Technology Center; Bowie State College.

Hagerstown (pop. 35,445). Industrial and transportation hub of western Maryland; engines and transmissions; industrial machinery; printing; travel trailers; apparel; credit-card processing; Jonathan Hager House; Hagerstown Junior College.

Annapolis (pop. 33,187).

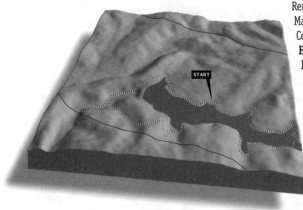

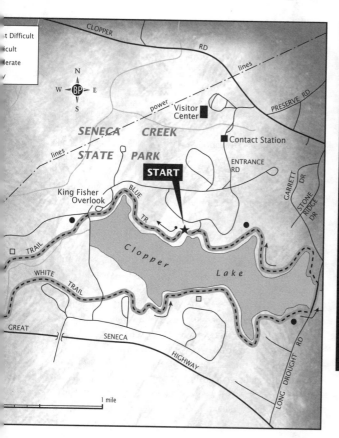

Ride Information

Trail Maintenance Hotline:
Maryland Forest, Park, and Wildlife Service
(301) 924-2127

Schedule:
Park is open every day
April through September, 8 a.m. to dusk
October through March, 10 a.m. to dusk

Maps:
USGS maps: Germantown, MD; Gaithersburg, MD
ADC Maps: Montgomery County road map
DeLorme: Maryland/Delaware Atlas & Gazetteer – Page 56 D-2
Seneca Creek State Park trail map

State capital on Severn River; communications; electronic engineering services; insurance; seafood processing; boat building; Maryland State House; United States Naval Academy; St. John's College.

Cumberland (pop. 23,706). Industrial center of western Maryland; fine printing papers; blankets; clothing; boats; plastic containers; testing and production of guided missile equipment; Chesapeake and Ohio Canal National Historic Park; History House; George Washington's Headquarters.

College Park (pop. 21,927). Suburb of Washington, DC; communications equipment; engineering, architectural, and surveying services; main campus of the University of Maryland.

Greenbelt (pop. 21,096). Suburb of Washington, DC.

Large unincorporated communities, suburbs of Baltimore and Washington, DC, include: **Silver Spring** (pop. 76,046); **Dundalk** (pop. 65,800); **Bethesda** (pop. 62,936); **Columbia** (pop. 75,883); **Towson** (pop. 49,445); **Wheaton-Glenmont** (pop. 53,720); **Aspen Hill** (pop. 45,494); **Essex** (pop. 40,872); and **Glen Burnie** (pop. 37,305)

Mckeldin Area

Ride Specs

Start: Switchback Trail trail-head

Length: 5.0 miles

Rating: Easy to Moderate

Terrain: Hard dirt/single-track trails

Other Uses: Hiking, horseback riding

Getting There

From the **Baltimore Beltway (695)** – Take **I-70 west.** Go 8.5 miles to **Exit 83 Marriottsville Road north.** Follow Marriottsville Road north for 4 miles, passing through Marriottsville. The **Mckeldin Area park entrance** road is on the right. Turn **right** on the park entrance road and follow it uphill to the parking area.

The Switchback Trail through the Mckeldin Area is a perfect example of the "classic ride" if ever there was one. It begins as a well maintained, packed dirt and gravel trail all the way down to the river. Along the way serene forested surroundings isolate you from the daily grind and hectic world of the Washington-Baltimore area, transporting you deep into a peaceful wilderness. Once you reach the picturesque south branch of the Patapsco River, Switchback Trail becomes a fun and challenging single-track; rugged yet well maintained. Nearing the end of the ride, after a respite along the river's banks, you will be confronted with the ultimate challenge, as the trail turns sharply left and goes vertical. There are no ways around this steep obstacle. Even walking up can be a real task. This isn't to say that riding up this section of trail is impossible, though, and I issue this challenge to anyone willing to go for it.

The Mckeldin Area is a unique stop along the Patapsco Valley State Park. It's nudged into the southeast corner of Carroll County where the North Branch and the South Branch of the Patapsco River converge. The beautiful Liberty Lake, one of Baltimore's primary water supplies, fills the valley just north of Mckeldin. Liberty Lake was created by damming the North Branch less than one mile from Switchback Trail.

Switchback Trail is open to hikers, bikers, and equestrians alike, and is quite popular throughout the year. Fortunately, the trail's design is well suited for all those wishing to enjoy its delightful scenery, and can accommodate them well. However, cyclists should be very alert and pass with caution when sharing

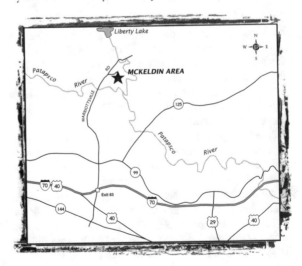

MilesDirections

0.0 START from the main entrance road at the information/toll booth. The trailhead is just off the road with a clearly marked sign reading "SWITCHBACK TRAIL, 5 MILES." You will follow this white-blazed trail the whole way through the park.

0.5 Come to the end of the descent.

0.6 At the fork in the trail, stay left, following the much larger Switchback Trail. Climb for about 0.2 miles. The trail then changes to rolling terrain.

1.2 Pass a small shelter on the right and a minor trail turning left up to the ballfield. Stay right, continuing on Switchback Trail.

1.6 Come to the end of another good descent. Stay left, continuing on Switchback Trail.

1.8 Cross the paved park road. Switchback Trail picks up directly across the road and changes to all singletrack. It follows some difficult rollers before racing all the way downhill to the Patapsco River.

2.0 Reach the bottom of the descent. At the river, turn left on Switchback Trail, riding downstream with the river.

3.0 Stay right, continuing along the North Branch River.

3.9 Turn hard left away from the river and attempt to ride straight up this vertical climb.

(continues on next page)

MilesDirections*(continued)*

4.0 Reach the top of the hill. Turn right, continuing to follow the White Blaze at the top. Note the wooden trail post here.

4.4 Reach the asphalt road. Follow this all the way back around to the parking area.

5.0 Reach the parking lot.

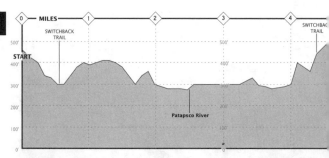

trails with horseback riders. Remember also to smile and be courteous to all the hikers who are there to enjoy the same spoils of nature that the Mckeldin Area has to offer.

In Addition...

•Formed by the junction of the North and South branches west of Baltimore, the Patapsco River, flows southeast for 65 miles to the Chesapeake Bay.

•Maryland is comprised of 23 counties, one independent city (Baltimore), and has a population of 5,006,265 people in 1997, all of whom live within its 9,775 square miles of land.

•Patapsco State Park's Mckeldin Area is situated at the junction of Carroll County, Howard County, and Baltimore County

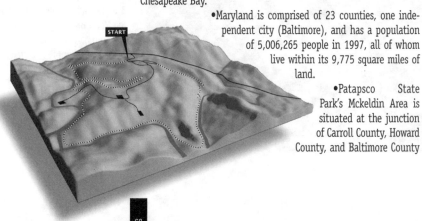

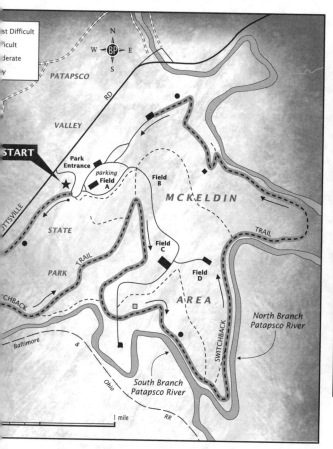

Ride Information

Trail Maintenance Hotline:
Patapsco Valley State Park HQ
(410) 461-5005
Emergency 24 hrs
(410) 461-0050
TTD
(301) 974-3683

Costs:
$2.00 on weekends and holidays

Schedule:
Open from 10 a.m. to sunset,
Thursday – Sunday

Maps:
USGS maps: Sykesville, MD
ADC Maps: Carroll County,
    Baltimore County road maps
DeLorme: Maryland/Delaware Atlas
    & Gazetteer – Page 57 A-5
Patapsco Valley State Park trail map

just on the edge of Maryland's Coastal Plain and its Piedmont Plateau. The Piedmont is a rolling upland, about 40 miles in width and includes the Frederick Valley, which is drained by the Monocacy River.

•Maryland's longest river is the Potomac, flowing east along the state's southern border. The primary eastward-flowing rivers north of the Potomac are the Patuxent, Severn, Patapsco, and Susquehanna. Each of these rivers, and most of those on the Eastern Shore, enter the Chesapeake Bay.

•The Potomac River has its origins in northeast West Virginia, flowing nearly 285 miles along the Virginia-Maryland border into the Chesapeake Bay. It is navigable by large ships as far inland as Washington, DC.

Avalon Area

Ride Specs

Length: 12 miles
Rating: Moderate to Difficult
Terrain: Mostly rugged singletrack with some pavement
Other Uses: Hiking, horseback riding

Getting There

From **Washington** – Take **I-95 north** to **Exit 47, Route 195 east (towards BWI airport)**. Take the first exit onto **Route 1 (Exit 3 – Washington Blvd)** and turn **right** heading **south**. Take the first right and immediately take the **first left** into **Patapsco State Valley Park.** Follow this road to the "T" intersection and turn right towards the **Glen Artney Area.** Make your first left and park at the **far parking lot** by the fishing pond.

Known simply as the Avalon Area by most cyclists, this small corner of Patapsco State Park is quite possibly one of Washington/Baltimore's most popular mountain biking playgrounds. Avalon's terrain is oftentimes severe and nearly always challenging, but for serious off-roaders, these conditions represent nothing less than prime mountain biking.

The ride begins at the Vineland trailhead (purple) off of the Glen Artney parking lot. After a short climb the trail quickly takes you barreling downhill along twisting singletrack toward the river. At one point further along this trail, you'll pass through a virtually pure beech forest which, in late autumn, resembles a tunnel of thick gold. Enjoy Gristmill Trail (green) while you can, because this flat, paved path, which takes you over Patapsco's famous Swinging Bridge is but a brief respite before the challenges of the Orange Grove Area.

Like the beginning of the ride, the terrain through the Orange Grove Area becomes quite severe. Much of the Blue Trail is steep and rocky, a good reason why it's considered a prime location for off-road races throughout the season. After negotiating the near vertical descent back to the river, the ride returns, for the most part, along the same route. Before you head home, however, take the time to see the cascades just up the river from the Swinging Bridge.

It's worth noting that the course selected for this book is only one of a countless number of routes within the Avalon Area. At the time *The Washington/Baltimore Mountain Bike Book* went to press, Patapsco's fantastic network of trails were all open to

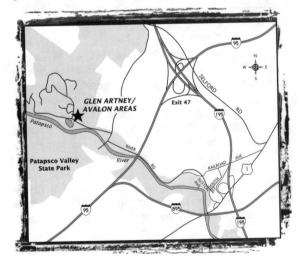

MilesDirections

0.0 START from the Glen Artney Parking lot, pedaling north away from the pond. Ride along the road through the tunnel. Bear right at the fork. Do not head up on the road.

0.2 Shortly before the metal railings, turn left on Vineland Trail (purple). This trail is blazed in white squares with a purple dot in the middle.

0.4 Reach a trail intersection and turn left, then immediately turn right on the road. Continue on the road for approximately two-tenths of a mile, then bear right toward the picnic area. Go through the small gate and continue on the gravel road.

0.7 Bear right on the singletrack beneath the power lines. Continue straight.

0.8 Reach an intersection in the trail and continue straight toward the ruins on the left.

0.9 Reach the fire road. Continue straight.

1.7 Go through the tunnel beneath the railroad tracks and immediately turn right on the paved path (green).

2.8 Turn left, crossing over the river on the swinging bridge. Immediately after crossing the bridge, turn left on River Road (paved).

3.0 Turn right on Ridge Trail (orange) and continue uphill. The entrance to this forest road is marked with a "No Parking" sign.

3.1 Make a sharp right-handed U-turn onto singletrack, continuing to follow the orange blazes.

(continues on next page)

mountain bikes with no significant challenges to its access. Along with Avalon's proximity to Baltimore, it's easy to understand why this ideal section of parkland is so popular among off-road cyclists. The area's popularity does, however, raise some concerns regarding overuse and trail damage. Hundreds of cyclists, hikers, and equestrians may crowd this trail system on any given weekend, making trail maintenance a very serious issue, not to men-

MilesDirections *(continued)*

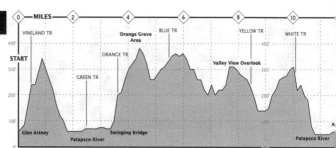

3.4 Turn left at this intersection, following the blue blazes. Cascade Branch Creek parallels the trail on the right. Follow the Blue Trail south toward Landing Road.

3.6 Turn right across the creek at the small outcropping of rocks. Continue following the blue blazes.

5.0 You should be riding parallel to Landing Road (paved) at this point.

5.25 Turn left on Norris Road (dirt). Look for the trailhead on the right.

5.3 Turn right at the trailhead on the blue-blazed trail. Get ready for a short, fast descent.

5.7 Reach an intersection. Continue straight, following the Red Trail.

5.9 Reach a small sign with red, white, and blue markers. Continue straight, following the blue-blazed trail.

6.4 Make a sharp, right-handed U-turn, continuing down the singletrack. The trail is now blazed blue/orange.

6.75 Turn left on the Valley View Trail (white blaze).

6.9 Reach the Valley View Overlook.

7.1 Turn right on the Orange Trail.

7.11 Turn left on the Blue Trail after a short ascent, then head downhill past two sets of ruins. Continue bearing left along this trail.

7.26 Turn left at this intersection pedaling through an open field.

7.5 Re-enter the woods and enjoy the twisting singletrack.

8.3 Turn right at this intersection following the yellow blazes. This trail marks the park's boundary.

(continues on next page)

tion a serious challenge. In order to maintain access to this priceless off-road habitat make sure you get involved with local clubs, organizations, park officials, and other trail users to help preserve the trails and the integrity of the Avalon Area. You may, otherwise, find it necessary to pull these pages from the book and use them as kindling. Without trail access, these maps become about as useless as aerodynamic handlebars on a mountain bike.

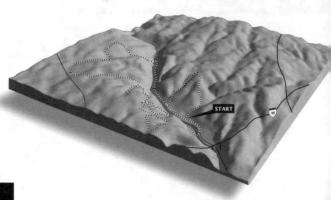

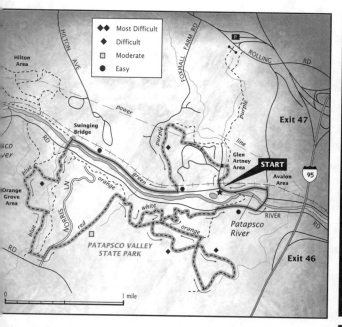

Ride Information

Trail Maintenance Hotline:
Patapsco Valley State Park HQ
(410) 461-5005
Emergency 24 hrs
(410) 461-0050
TTD (301) 974-3683

Schedule:
Open from 10 a.m. to sunset,
Thursday – Sunday

Maps:
USGS maps: Sykesville, MD
ADC Maps: Carroll County,
 Baltimore County road maps
DeLorme: Maryland/Delaware Atlas
 & Gazetteer – Page 58 C-1
Patapsco Valley State Park trail map

Miles Directions (continued)

8.4 Make a sharp right turn up the steep climb. Good luck!

8.6 Turn right at this trail intersection.

9.4 Continue straight through this intersection.

9.5 Bear left at this intersection and prepare to climb. This trail is blazed orange.

10.0 Reach the intersection of the white and orange trails. Turn right on the white trail.

10.8 Reach the bottom of the descent. Turn right on River Road.

11.3 Turn left at this intersection crossing over the river.

11.5 Turn left at this intersection following the road back to the Glen Artney Area.

11.9 Reach the parking area.

Northern Central Rail Trail

Ride Specs

Start: Ashland parking lot
Length: 19.7 miles one way
Rating: Moderate
Terrain: Flat; hard-packed dirt trail
Other Uses: Hiking, horseback riding

Getting There

From the **Baltimore Beltway (695)** – Take **I-83 North** 5.5 miles to **Exit 20 (Shawan Road)**. Go east on Shawan Road less than one mile, then turn **right** on **Route 45 (York Road)**. Go one mile and turn **left** on **Ashland Road.** Follow Ashland Road 1.5 miles, passing **Hunt Valley Shopping Center** on your left. **Stay right** on Ashland Road **(do not bear left on Paper Mill Road)** to the parking lot for the **Northern Central Railroad Trail.**

Back when rails were king, the Northern Central Railroad was among the few rail lines dominating the Mid-Atlantic, carrying everything from milk, coal, and U.S. Mail to Presidents of the United States. For nearly 134 years the Northern Central Railroad was the locomotive link that carved its way through Maryland's hilly Piedmont region and Pennsylvania's rolling farmlands. It connected Baltimore with Gettysburg, York, and Harrisburg, Pennsylvania.

Scores of small towns sprang up along the line, prospering from Northern Central's service to the large cities. Such towns as Freeland, Bentley Springs, Parkton, Whitehall, Monkton, Corbett, Phoenix, and Ashland all sent their flour, milk, paper, coal, textiles, and other goods to Baltimore markets.

The Northern Central also served in the Civil War, carrying wounded soldiers from the bloody battlefields of Gettysburg south to Baltimore hospitals. Abraham Lincoln rode the rail line north to Gettysburg to deliver his famous Gettysburg Address. It later carried him back through Gettysburg on an agonizing trip to Harrisburg where he was buried following his assassination in April 1865 at Ford's Theater in Washington, DC.

The rail's rich history began to recede with the advent of trucks and automobiles, and in 1959 the Northern Central had to give up its local passenger service. But it was Agnes, the powerful hurricane of 1972, that dealt the final blow to the faltering rail line when it washed out and destroyed many of the railroad's bridges, ultimately knocking out remaining main-line passenger services and the line's important freight transportation. Northern Central Railroad's commercial success ended, but its new identity and prosperity were just beginning.

The rail line south of Cockeysville was purchased by the state of Maryland for freight service. This left the remaining line from Cockeysville north to the Pennsylvania border open for a unique and wonderful opportunity. The residents of Baltimore County realized this opportunity in 1980 when they pur-

chased the 20-mile corridor from Penn Central and began the back-breaking process of converting the rails to trails. After nine long, hard years of work and thousands of volunteers later, the Northern Central Rail Trail from Ashland to the Pennsylvania border was finished.

Now, more than 180,000 people visit and enjoy the trail each year. The Northern Central Rail Trail leads its visitors across Maryland's beautiful fields and meadows, past old forests and rural farmland, along the rushing waters of Little Falls and Gunpowder Falls, and through the many historic little towns whose whole history is based upon the corridor's connection between Baltimore and Harrisburg.

Be warned that this once quiet treasure is gaining tremendous popularity and parking is very limited during the prime outdoor months. Take this into account when you wish to travel the rail and get there early.

MilesDirections

0.0 START from the NCRR Trail parking lot in Ashland and travel north on the Northern Central Railroad Trail.

2.0 Pass through the town of Phoenix. Toilets, phone, parking on the left.

Sight of the Phoenix textile mill razed for Loch Raven Reservoir. The reservoir, when built in 1922, never reached the mill. The mill ruins survive, still above the water line.

4.0 Pass through the town of Sparks.

6.0 Pass through the historic Victorian village of Corbett. Listed on the National Registry of Historic Places.

7.5 Pass through Monkton, show-casing the renovated Monkton train station, now a museum and park office. Monkton is also listed on the National Registry of Historic Places. Restroom, telephones, and food available. Monkton Bike rental and repair shop just off the main path.

10.8 Pass through the village of Whitehall. Telephones and parking on the left. Whitehall is a former paper mill town that used the rail to export its paper to Baltimore.

12.9 Pass through Parkton. Parkton was the railroad's hub for exporting dairy products south to Baltimore.

15.7 Reach the historic resort town of Bentley Springs. Portable toilet available.

(continues on next page)

MilesDirections *(continued)*

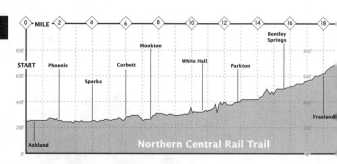

Northern Central Rail Trail

18.0 Pass through the town of Freeland. Restrooms and parking available.

19.7 Reach the Maryland/ Pennsylvania state border. From here, you must either have arranged a car shuttle back to the Ashland parking lot or you must ride back.

In Addition...

Rails-To-Trails Conservancy

The mission of the Rails-to-Trails Conservancy is to "enhance America's communities and countryside by converting thousands of miles of abandoned rail corridors and connecting open spaces into a nationwide network of public trails."

Every large city and small town in America, by the early twentieth century, was connected by steel and railroad ties. In 1916, the United States had laid nearly 300,000 miles of track across the country, giving it the distinction of having the world's largest rail system. Since then, other forms of transportation, such as cars, trucks, and airplanes have diminished the importance of the railroad and the country's impressive network of rail lines has shrunk to less than 150,000 miles of track. Railroad companies abandon more than 2,000 miles of track each year, leaving unused rail corridors overgrown and idle.

It wasn't until the mid-1960s that the idea to refurbish these abandoned rail corridors into useable footpaths and trails was introduced. And in 1963, work began in Chicago to build a 55-mile stretch of abandoned right-of-way into the Illinois Prairie Path. It took nearly two decades for the idea of converting old railways into useable footpaths to catch on. Then in 1986 the Rails-To-Trails Conservancy was founded, its mission specifically to help communities see their dreams of having a useable rail corridor for

START

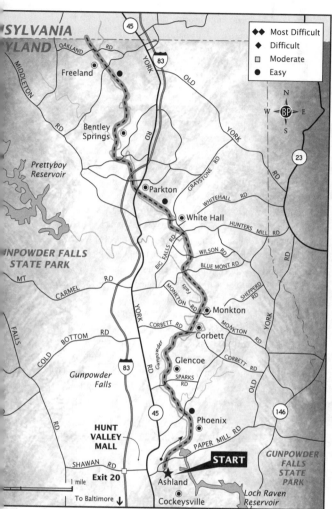

Ride Information

Trail Maintenance Hotline:
Gunpowder Falls State Park
(301) 592-2897
Rails-To-Trails Conservancy
(202) 797-5400

Local Bike Shops:
Monkton Bike Shop
1900 Monkton Road
Monkton, MD 21111

Maps:
USGS maps: Cockeysville, MD;
   Hereford, MD; Phoenix, MD; New
   Freedom, MD
ADC Maps:Baltimore County Road
   Map
DeLorme: Maryland/Delaware Atlas
   & Gazetteer – Page 75 D-5

Also Available:
Guide To The Northern Central Rail
Trail; $6.50 (postpaid) from
Howling Wolf Publications, 8630
Fenton St, Silver Spring, MD
20910; (301) 589-9455

recreation and non-motorized travel a reality. At the time the Conservancy began operations only 100 open rail-trails existed. Today, more than 500 trails are open to the public, totalling more than 5,000 miles of converted right-of-ways. The Rails-To-Trails Conservancy is currently working on more than 500 additional rails-to-trails projects.

Ultimately, their goal is to see a completely interconnected system of trails throughout the entire United States. If you're interested in learning more about rails-to-trails and wish to support the Conservancy, please write to the address in the back of the book.

Susquehanna State Park

Ride Specs

Start: Picnic area
Length: 7 miles
Rating: Moderate to Difficult
Terrain: Singletrack, paved roads
Other Uses: Hiking, horseback riding, fishing, boating.

T he setting for this ride is Susquehanna State Park, 30 miles north of Baltimore near the Pennsylvania state line. First inhabited by the Susquehannock Indians, this area later became a center for the Maryland and Pennsylvania Railroad. Today, all that remains of the railroad are abandoned structures from the past when the rail line helped the farms and quarries of Northern Harford County to prosper. Also present is a network of trails and recreation areas for folks to enjoy year-round.

This ride takes you along five of the Susquehanna State Park's many different trails. Cyclists will ride through the river valley, beneath heavy forest cover, and across wide-open fields. The ride also passes by Harford and Cecil Counties' only working gristmill, one of the many historic points of interest on this ride.

As you enter the park, you will clearly see evidence of the past. Take time for a walking tour of the gristmill area, or explore the park's several buildings, all of which were built between 1794 and 1815, including the Rock Run Gristmill, a springhouse, a carriage barn, and a tollhouse. Each of these unique and historic building offers a glimpse into the lifestyle of the 1800s.

This particular mountain bike tour travels past the Rock Run Gristmill. Built in 1794 by John Stump, a successful Harford County businessman, the mill served as the center of activity in the community. In addition to activities that provided milling services and buying and selling grain, the mill also housed the local post office. Still in operation today, the mill's most prominent feature is its 12-ton, 84-bucket wheel, powered by water running

Getting There

From **Baltimore** – Take **I-95 north to Exit 89 (Route 155 west)** toward Bel Air. Turn **right on Route 161 (Rock Run Road)** and follow the brown signs to the Rock Run Gristmill Historic Area. Turn **left at Stafford Road** toward the **Deer Creek Picnic Area.** As you drive into the picnic area, drive directly to the far right corner of the lot. The trails begin here.

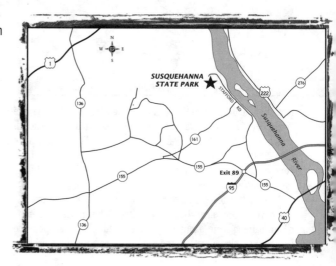

down Mill Race, a man-made stream draining from a small dammed pond on higher ground.

The power from the gristmill wheel's rotation operates a complex set of pulleys, belts, and gears that can be quickly adjusted by the miller to determine the grain's consistency. As you walk

inside the mill, pay close attention to the flood level markers, especially the one from 1889. It's hard to imagine that nearly the entire first floor of this structure was at one point completely submerged. Pictures of past floods, storms, and ice flows that greatly affected and shaped this area are also on display.

The next stop on the tour is the springhouse. Built in 1804, the house's main purpose was to cover drinking water used at the gristmill and to serve as a cold storage house for dairy products and foods. Continue to the carriage house and the "three holer," a small stone building adjacent to the carriage house. This structure was once an outhouse with accommodations for three people—thus the name "three holer."

The tollhouse, perhaps one of the most important buildings at the historic area, was built in the early 1800s as part of a project by the Rock Run Bridge and Bank Company. This included the one-mile bridge that crossed the Susquehanna River. Intended to replace the ferry as the primary means across the river, the bridge was used extensively from its completion in 1815 until 1823 when a fire destroyed it. The bridge was then rebuilt and reused for 20 more years until it was partially destroyed by the rhythmic motion of crossing cattle. A final blow to the bridge's integrity came in 1856 when a damaging ice flow down the river completely destroyed the bridge. If you look out on the river, you can still see the stone footings that once supported this structure, the first of its kind to span the Susquehanna.

MilesDirections

0.0 START at the picnic area from the intersection of the Red and Green Trails. A "walk zone" sign marks the entrance. Turn right and follow the green blazes.

1.0 Reach the point where you can see the intersection of Craig's Corner Road and Stafford Road. Continue following the green blazes. This is a popular access point for tubing down Deer Creek.

1.8 The intersection marked "White Oak" to the left will take you to a small opening where you can admire Maryland's state tree. This particular white oak grew from a small acorn at the time of the revolutionary war. This is a perfect spot for a water break or picnic.

1.9 Reach the intersection of the Green and Silver Trails. Continue straight through this intersection following the Silver Trail. The Green Trail continues to the left and heads back to the picnic/parking area where you initially parked.

2.1 Reach the Blue Trail. Turn right, cross the creek, and follow the blue blazes. This trail will take you out of the woods through an open field.

2.7 Just before the Blue Trail turns back into the woods, there is an orange trail marker in the ground directly beneath you. Turn right onto the Orange Trail and begin following the orange blazes.

(continues on next page)

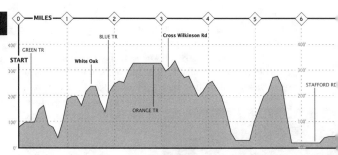

MilesDirections *(continued)*

3.1 Pass the park office and maintenance complex. Continue straight. This area also serves as the equestrian parking lot.

3.5 Reach the first intersection of the Orange (Ivy Branch) Trail and Wilkinson Road. Cross the road. The Orange Trail picks up directly on the other side. After a short ascent you will be treated to some of the best singletrack in the park. Continue following the orange blazes.

4.8 Reach an intersection with the Blue Trail. Continue straight, following the orange blazes. Ahead of you is a short twisty exciting descent.

5.1 Reach Wilkinson Road again. Turn right on Wilkinson Road, then immediately left on Rock Run Road. Head toward the Historic Area.

5.2 Turn left at the connection with the Red Trail. Follow the red blazes across the creek and get ready to climb.

(continues on next page)

The ditch adjacent to the mill and parallel to the river was once a very important canal that extended 45 miles from Havre de Grace to Wrightsville. The original Canal Company was chartered in 1783 and had the authority to purchase all the lands required for construction. Initially, it was intended for the canal to have grain warehouses and saw mills along its banks to accommodate the developing town of Baltimore. When completed, the canal was 20 feet wide and up to 12 feet deep. It contained 29 locks that raised and lowered boats from 29 feet at Havre de Grace to 1,000 feet at Wrightsville. With the flood of 1889, the canal suffered substantial damages and the Canal Company received extensive financial losses. Since then, the canal's usefulness faded and was no longer used. Today, all that is left of the canal within the park are three of its massive granite locks.

If your thirst for more information on the area's history has not been

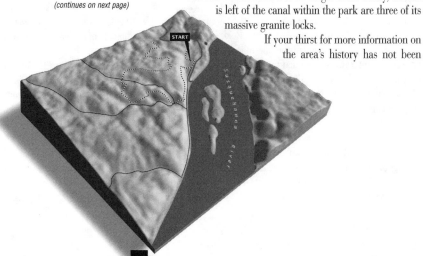

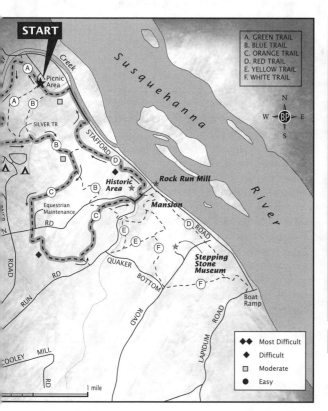

START

A. GREEN TRAIL
B. BLUE TRAIL
C. ORANGE TRAIL
D. RED TRAIL
E. YELLOW TRAIL
F. WHITE TRAIL

◆◆ Most Difficult
◆ Difficult
☐ Moderate
● Easy

1 mile

Ride Information

Trail Maintenance Hotline:
Susquehanna State Park
(410) 557-7994
Havre de Grace Chamber of
Commerce/Tourism Board:
(410) 939-3303

Schedule:
Day Use
dawn to sunset

Maps:
USGS maps: Conowingo Dam, MD-
PA; Delta, MD-PA
DeLorme: Maryland/Delaware Atlas
and Gazetteer – Page 76 A-3
Susquehanna State Park trail map

MilesDirections(continued)

6.3 Reach the intersection of
Stafford Road and the Red Trail.
Turn left and follow Stafford Road
for approximately three tenths of a
mile.
6.6 Turn left at the brown gate in
the open field and follow the Red
Trail toward the woods.
6.8 Cross the wooden bridge and
bear left, continuing to follow the
red blazes.
7.0 Reach the end of the ride.

quenched, you might consider visiting Havre de Grace and the Susquehanna Museum of Havre de Grace at the Lock House. Currently, the museum is going through an extensive restoration program. Its goal is to recreate a working lock to help people fully understand and interpret the canal's operations. In addition, a display house is envisioned to show preserved gates, artifacts, and information on the local history of Havre de Grace and surrounding Tidewater, Maryland. There are also four other museums, numerous shops, and fine restaurants along the promenade and waterfront as well as several historic homes, some of which have been converted into wonderful bed and breakfasts.

L.F.Cosca Regional Park

Ride Specs

Start: Clearwater Nature Center
Length: 5+ miles of trails
Rating: Easy to moderate
Terrain: Singletrack
Other Uses: Hiking, Nature Center, Nature Trails

Getting There

From the **Capital Beltway (495)** – Take **Exit 7** to **MD-Route 5 South (Branch Ave) toward Waldorf.** Go approximately 4 miles to **Route 223 (Woodyard Road).** Turn right on Woodyard Road, taking this 0.6 miles to Brandywine Road. Turn **left on Brandywine Road.** Follow this south toward Clinton 0.75 miles, then turn **right on Thrift Road.** Thrift Road takes you south 1.5 miles to the park entrance on your right. Go right into the park to the **Clearwater Nature Center** on top of the hill. Parking, telephone, toilets, and small creatures at the nature center.

T hings can often deceive you, then disappoint you, and leave you feeling short-changed. Louise F. Cosca Regional Park, just outside the town of Clinton in Prince George's County, Maryland, is one such place that will, indeed, deceive you. It will not, however, leave you disappointed. For, despite its small size, this park has everything an off-road cyclist can dream of: deep, wooded surroundings; stream crossings; a beautiful 15-acre lake; quick, rugged singletrack trails; and a variety of off-road route possibilities.

Your ride starts from the parking lot at Clearwater Nature Center, one of the state's most unique and innovative nature centers. This lava-rock building is placed deep within the woods, featuring a large greenhouse and indoor pond, complete with live occupants. From here, you'll descend quickly into the woods along the park's main trail. (Although this book guides you left, following trails around the perimeter of the park, don't hesitate to explore and create your own circuits.) The trail travels quickly along the creek, oftentimes precariously close to the water's edge, then up through the trees above the creek valley. This, of course, is leading up to a thrilling, narrow descent down winding singletrack to Butler Creek. Crossing Butler Creek presents a challenge though, as it is a bit too wide to jump and somewhat difficult to negotiate from the bike. While descending the last hill, detour right onto "Trail C" and take the easy route over the creek via a small wooden bridge at the north end of the lake. Once across the creek, the ride just gets better. Whichever route you choose

MilesDirections

0.0 START from the parking lot at the Clearwater Nature Center and follow Trail A down wooden-plank steps into the woods.

0.1 Turn left at this trail intersection with Trail B. Turning right takes you along a secondary trail toward the Group Pavilion. Heading straight on Trail B takes you up a steep hill to the lake.

0.8 You may either continue straight on Trail B down this fantastic descent or turn right on Trail C then left on Trail H. The strategy is to connect with Trail D. The advantage of detouring on Trail C then left on Trail H back to Trail D is that you avoid slogging through thick brush and Butler Branch Creek, over which there is no good place to cross. Take your pick!

1.0 Bear left on Trail D. This is an exciting trail, taking you up and down on a quick and challenging singletrack. Trail E is a fun alternative here, twisting quickly through the woods along a more level terrain.

1.5 Turn right on Trail F. This trail gently rolls along a more open jeep trail.

2.0 Cross Thrift Road. Continue on Trail F.

(continues on next page)

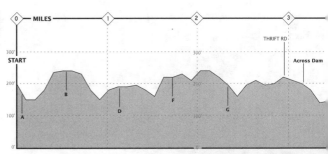

MilesDirections(continued)

2.7 Turn right at the power lines (Trail G).

2.9 Turn left on Thrift Road. You could follow the power lines (Trail G) all the way back into the park.

3.1 Bear right off Thrift Road to a hiking trail, which takes you past the Group Pavilion and up to the dam.

3.3 Reach the lake. Cross the dam, taking Trail B down the hill back to Trail A.

A good diversion at the lake—turn right to the snack bar for some food.

3.5 Follow Trail A back up the hill to the Clearwater Nature Center parking lot.

toward the west end of the park, you're in for a wonderful ride. The trails twist back and forth beneath the tall trees and, in the fall season, can be breathtaking. Continuing around the perimeter of the park, the trails roll more gently back toward the start of the ride, allowing you to sit back and enjoy your wooded surroundings.

The variety of possible routes within Cosca's 500 acres of rolling, wooded parkland will turn your ride into much more than a quick jaunt through the woods. You can spend hours exploring the different trails, then pedal over to the snack bar and finish a great day by lounging along the shores of L.F. Cosca's lake.

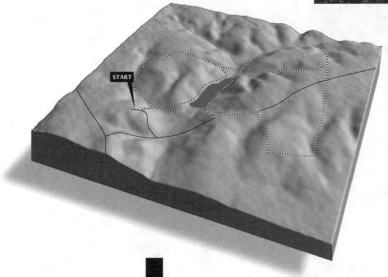

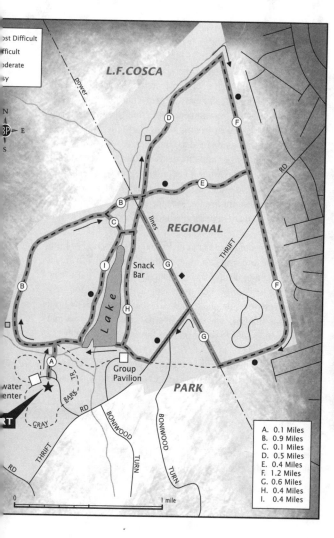

Trail Maintenance Hotline:
L.F. Cosca Regional Park
(301) 868-1397
Clearwater Nature Center
(301) 297-4575

Costs:
Memorial Day to Labor Day: non-residents of Prince George's or Montgomery Counties must pay a $5.00 fee for parking within the confines of the park.

Schedule:
Open daily 7:30 a.m. to dusk, year-round.

Maps:
USGS maps: Piscataway, MD
ADC Maps: Prince George's County road map
DeLorme: Maryland/Delaware Atlas and Gazetteer – Page 37 B-5
Park service trail map

A. 0.1 Miles
B. 0.9 Miles
C. 0.1 Miles
D. 0.5 Miles
E. 0.4 Miles
F. 1.2 Miles
G. 0.6 Miles
H. 0.4 Miles
I. 0.4 Miles

Cedarville State Park

H ere's an off-road ride that rolls along forest roads and wooded trails through Prince George's and Charles Counties' quiet state forest. There are no monuments, natural wonders, or sights of great historical significance in Cedarville State Forest, and even the name may leave you wondering, as cedars are uncommon to the immediate area. (The name, in fact, was taken from a nearby post office.) What this small state forest in southern Maryland does have is a network of wonderful wooded trails and dirt roads to guide you beneath tall stands of loblolly and white pine, around groves of holly and magnolia trees, past a four-acre lake, through the headwaters of Maryland's largest freshwater swamp, and across abandoned farmland with streams and springs once used for making "moonshine."

The state acquired the land in 1930 during a period of farm abandonment and crop failures in southern Maryland. It planned to use this land to demonstrate techniques in forestry, but is now managed as a place for both recreation and business. You may notice, as you ride through the park, sizeable areas that have been clear-cut or thinned. The cut timber, restricted to Virginia and loblolly pine, is sold to paper mills as far away as West Virginia and Pennsylvania.

This is a wonderful ride for novices and experts alike who have a passion for the great outdoors. Cedarville's terrain is mostly flat, as is most of southern Maryland, but the beauty of its wooded forest roadways rise high above most everything else in the area.

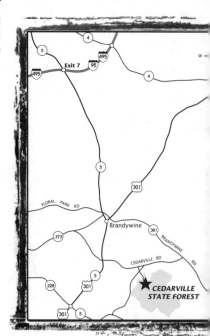

0.0 START at Cedarville State Forest's park office on Bee Oak Road. From the parking lot, turn right on Bee Oak Road (paved).
0.1 Turn right on Hidden Springs Road (paved).
0.7 Hidden Springs Road comes to an end. Turn left on Sunset Road. This is a rolling rutted dirt trail through the woods. (Fish Hatchery to the right at this intersection.)
1.7 Turn right on Forest Road (dirt road).
2.8 Pass Cedarville Pond on the left. Go straight through the steel gate, continuing on Forest Road.
3.1 Turn right off of Forest Road on Plantation Trail (Brown Trail), which loops around the south end of the park.

The Civilian Conservation Corps planted the thick growth of loblolly pine that this trail tunnels through in the 1930s.

3.6 Plantation Trail comes to a "T," intersecting with Swamp Trail (Green Trail). Turn left, continuing to follow the Brown Trail signs.
4.0 Turn left on Forest Road (dirt road).
4.7 Pass Cedarville Pond on the right.

(continues on next page)

In Addition...

There are five natural regions in the state of Maryland rising from sea level in the east along the Chesapeake Bay to more than 3,000 feet in the western Allegheny Mountains.

The Coastal Plain covers the eastern half of the state from the Delmarva Peninsula through southern Maryland. This tidewater area is low and flat and is cut by lots of streams. At the center of Maryland's coastal plain is the Chesapeake Bay, which separates southern Maryland on the west and the peninsula on the east.

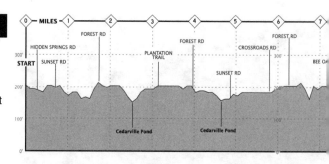

MilesDirections*(continued)*

4.8 Turn right on Mistletoe Road (doubletrack trail).

Watch for the brown wooden street signs at each intersection along Forest Road.

5.1 Continue straight through the wooden gate on Mistletoe Road.
5.8 Turn left on Crossroads Road at this intersection (doubletrack trail).
5.9 Cross Heritage Trail. Continue straight on Crossroads Road.
6.3 Turn right on Forest Road (dirt road).
7.2 Turn left on Bee Oak Road (paved).
7.9 Reach the Park Office.

The Piedmont Plateau lies just west of Maryland's Coastal Plain. These two regions are separated by a fall line of rivers. The fall line marks a drop in land level often marked by waterfalls. This line extends from the head of the Chesapeake Bay southwest through Baltimore and Washington, DC. The Piedmont Plateau is about 40 miles wide and rolls upland toward the western mountains. Included in Maryland's Piedmont Plateau is the Frederick Valley, which is drained by the Monocacy River.

The Blue Ridge extends across Maryland from north to south along the Frederick-Washington county line. The Blue Ridge is a range of the Appalachian Mountain chain and extends from southern Pennsylvania to northern Georgia. In Maryland, the eastern end of the Blue Ridge Mountains is Catoctin Mountain, a section of the Blue Ridge extending from the Pennsylvania border south to Virginia. Camp David is located in this part of Maryland.

The Valley and Ridge region of Maryland occupies part of the narrow neck of western Maryland. Its outstanding feature is Hagerstown, just north of Frederick. Hagerstown is a manufacturing center located in the fertile Cumberland Valley.

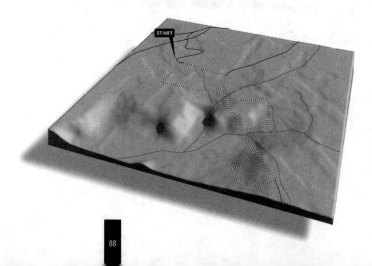

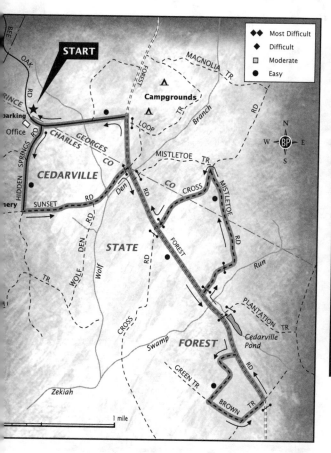

Ride Information

Trail Maintenance Hotline:
Maryland Forest, Park, and Wildlife
Service
(301) 888-1622

Schedule:
Open every day 8 a.m. to sunset
most of the year. Winter schedule:
10 a.m. to sunset

Maps:
USGS maps: Brandywine, MD;
   Hughesville, MD
ADC Maps: Prince George's County
   road map, Charles County road
   map
DeLorme: Maryland/Delaware Atlas
   and Gazetteer – Page 37 D-6
Park Service trail map

The Appalachian Plateau covers Maryland's extreme western panhandle. Running northeast-southeast, the Appalachian Plateau is made up of a series of parallel mountain ranges and thick-forested valleys all within the Allegheny Mountains. Backbone Mountain, Maryland's highest peak, rises to 3,360 feet in this area.

Maryland is one of the country's smaller states, measuring only 10,577 square miles—this compared to Virginia's 40,817 square miles or Texas' 267,338 square miles. Despite its size, however, Maryland enjoys an abundance of natural resources, with fertile soil, valuable mineral deposits, and a thriving seafood industry. Nearly 50 percent of the land is forested, with pine and oak dominating the coastal region, while mixed hardwoods fill in the rest of the state.

Patuxent River Park

Ride Specs

Start: Park Office
Length: 7 miles
Rating: Easy to moderate
Terrain: singletrack
Other Uses: Nature trail, history, hiking, hunting, horseback riding

T he ride through this section of the Patuxent River Park is a fantastic journey over its wooded, rolling terrain on nearly 10 miles of woodland horse trails and twisting singletrack. The trails, open to hikers, horseback riders, and cyclists, lead you through Jug Bay's beautiful 2,000-acre "limited-use natural area," and provide a close-up look at a coastal ecosystem in one of Maryland's premier greenways.

Acquired by the Maryland Department of Natural Resources, the Jug Bay Natural Area represents the nationally acclaimed land preservation program of the state of Maryland called Program Open Space. This program was designed to preserve open-space land and to protect valuable natural resources.

The results of this program offer something of value to all who come and visit. Naturalists are given the unique opportunity to observe freshwater, tidal, and nontidal wetlands; historians may exhibit life along the river during the nineteenth century at The Patuxent Village; nature lovers can drive a four-mile, self-guided tour through the Merkle Wildlife Sanctuary, including the thousand-foot boardwalk crossing the Mattaponi Creek; hunters enjoy bow season for squirrel, rabbit, and deer; hikers and equestrians have miles of trails; and most

Getting There

From the **Capital Beltway (495)** – Take **Exit 11 east** on **Route 4 east (Pennsylvania Avenue).** Follow **Route 4 east 6.3 miles,** then exit **left** on **Old Crain Highway south**. Almost immediately, turn left on **Croom Station Road.** Go **2.5 miles** and turn **left on Croom Road (Route 382).** Go 1.3 miles and turn **left on Croom Airport Road.** This takes you into **Patuxent River Park.** After two miles turn **left** on **Park Entrance Road** and travel 1.5 miles to the end, parking at the **Park Office.**

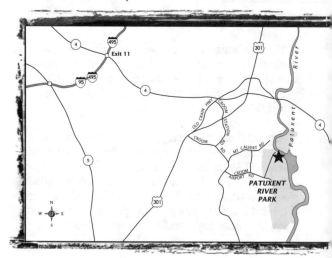

MilesDirections

0.0 START from the Park Office at the northern end of Park Entrance Road. Travel south on Park Entrance Road.

0.4 Turn right off Park Entrance Road through a wooden gate on Mount Calvert Horse Trail. The trail is slightly hidden from the road. A wooden post with a horse trail symbol marks the trailhead.

1.2 Turn left off Mount Calvert Horse Trail on Chapman Hiking Trail. This trail leads you away from a field into the woods.

1.6 Exit the woods around a steel gate and turn right on Park Entrance Road. Look for the yellow horse crossing sign just up the road.

1.7 Turn left on the Lonesome Pine Horse Trail just past the yellow horse crossing sign. A wooden post marks this trail with the horse trail symbol on it.

2.0 Turn right at this trail intersection, continuing downhill. Be careful of the wooden water bars laid across the trail.

2.3 Turn right at this trail intersection, continuing on the Lonesome Pine Horse Trail. Turning left takes you for a hilly ride along another horse trail to Croom Airport Road. This trail is often closed during wet seasons.

2.6 Turn left on Croom Airport Road. You should see the yellow horse crossing sign to the left up the road. Keep your eyes open for this trail.

(continues on next page)

MilesDirections *(continued)*

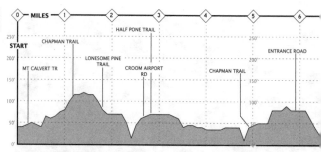

2.7 Turn right on the Half Pone Horse Trail. This trail is a bit obscure. Keep your eyes open for the wooden post that marks it.
3.2 Cross the dirt jeep trail, continuing straight on Half Pone Horse Trail.
3.5 Cross another dirt road. Follow Half Pone Horse Trail along the perimeter of the group campgrounds. The camp grounds and picnic area should be on your left. Continue following the trail around the right side of the cornfields. You will continue along what seems more like a tractor path around the cornfields until it dumps you back on Croom Airport Road next to Selby's Landing boat ramp.
4.6 Pass the gravel road and gate on the right.

(continues on next page)

important, off-road bicyclists are welcome. All hikers and riders, however, are required to register at the park office and have a park permit before venturing onto its trails. This is simple though, and permits can be obtained at the start of this ride from the park office for $2.00 a visit. A seasonal visitor's pass is also available.

This fabulous ride offers cyclists wanting to venture off the road and into the woods a fantastic opportunity to see nature up close without the grueling pressures of steep climbs and treacherous descents. Don't be fooled though. Patuxent River Park is full of exciting trails to keep cyclists of any ability interested and entertained.

In Addition...

Chesapeake Bay

Certainly, one of the most prominent features in this region is the Chesapeake Bay—the largest inlet on the Atlantic coast of the United States. The unique character and identity of eastern Maryland and Virginia are woven inexplicably around the bay's coastal environment and economy, giving this region a flavor all its own.

The Patuxent River, along which this ride is located, travels nearly 100 miles to reach the bay, and is one of the many broad, deep tidal rivers to pour into this vast waterway. Other major rivers feeding the bay are the Susquehanna, Patapsco, Severn, Potomac, Rapahannock, York, and James. The Chesapeake Bay is actually the "drowned" river valley of the lower part of the Susquehanna River, which pours into the Bay at its head near the Maryland/Pennsylvania border.

In all, the bay measures nearly 195 miles long, ranges from three to 25 miles wide, and is deep enough to accom-

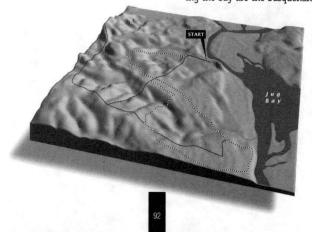

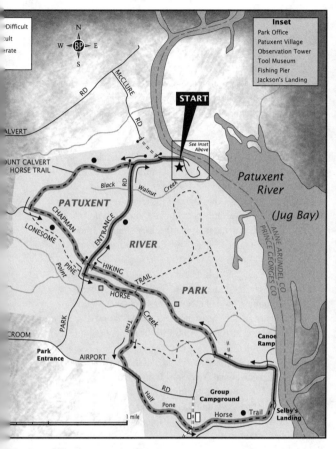

Difficult
ult
rate

N
W—BP—E
S

Inset
Park Office
Patuxent Village
Observation Tower
Tool Museum
Fishing Pier
Jackson's Landing

MCCLURE RD
RD

START

See Inset
Above

★

LVERT

)UNT CALVERT
HORSE TRAIL

Black RD
Walnut Creek

Patuxent
River

(Jug Bay)

PATUXENT

CHAPMAN

LONESOME

ENTRANCE

PINE
Point

HIKING

TRAIL

RIVER

HORSE

PARK

Creek

ANNE ARUNDEL CO.
PRINCE GEORGES CO.

Trail

CROOM

PARK

Park
Entrance

AIRPORT

Canoe
Ramp

RD

Half

Pone

Group
Campground

Horse   Trail

Selby's
Landing

1 mile

Ride Information

Trail Maintenance Hotline:
Patuxent River Park
(301) 627-6074

Costs
*Required park use permit (available
at park office) You may purchase
seasonal visitors pass; or pay $2.00
per visit.*

Schedule:
*Open daily, 8 a.m. to dusk
Park Office open: 8 a.m. to 4 p.m.*

Maps:
*USGS maps: Bristol, MD
ADC Maps: Prince George's
   County road map
DeLorme: Maryland/Delaware Atlas
   and Gazetteer – Page 38 A-1
Dept. of Parks & Rec. trail map
Patuxent River Park trail map*

MilesDirections(continued)

4.9 Turn right off Croom Airport
Road back into the woods on the
horse trail. This trailhead is very
obscure and overgrown. It begins
down off the road behind the
weeds and is marked by a wooden
horse trail post. There is a post on
opposite sides of Croom Airport
Road at this point.

5.7 Reach the trail intersection and
continue straight.

6.0 Turn right on Park Entrance
Road. You can, of course, go
straight on the hiking trail if you'd
like.

7.0 Arrive back at the Park Office.
Grab a soda and ride down to Jug
Bay for some rest.

modate oceangoing vessels. Its has about 27,000 miles of shoreline
and covers 3,237 square miles of water. The Chesapeake Bay is considered one of the most important commercial and sport fishing
grounds of the United States, and is famous for its oysters, crabs, and
diamondback terrapin.

Another unique feature associated with the bay is the
Chesapeake Bay Bridge-Tunnel, stretching between Cape Charles (the
southern tip of Virginia's Eastern Shore) and a point east of Norfolk,
Virginia. The bridge-tunnel carries motorists over and under 17.6
miles of uninterrupted ocean.

One of the nice things about traveling to the Patuxent River Park
is the classic eastern Maryland scenery and character that you are
bound to experience along the way. As you drive down Route 301,
you should have plenty of opportunities to purchase fresh blue crabs
from roadside vendors or stop at one of the many seafood restaurants.

Saint Mary's River Park

Ride Specs

Start: Main parking lot at the boat ramp
Length: 8.15 miles
Rating: Easy to Moderate
Terrain: Singletrack
Other Uses: Hiking, fishing, sailing

Getting There

From **Waldorf** – Take **Route 5 south to Leonardtown.** Continue for approximately five miles and turn **left on Camp Cosoma Road** (follow signs to **Saint Mary's River State Park**). Follow Camp Cosoma Road until it ends. Park at the far right corner (as you drive in) by the rest rooms. A sign marks the trailhead.

Southern Maryland does not usually conjure up images of great mountain biking terrain. However, near Lexington Park, north of Saint Mary's City in Saint Mary's County is a small treasure not too many off-road cyclists know about—Saint Mary's River State Park. Located between Leonardtown and Lexington Park, down near the mouth of the Chesapeake Bay, this remote park boasts over eight miles of pristine singletrack.

Designated a national historic landmark, making a short trip to Saint Mary's City is well worth the time. On March 25, 1634, some two hundred colonists sent by Lord Baltimore of England landed on the shores of Saint Clements Island. Two days later, they sailed their ships—the Ark and the Dove—up what is now the Saint Mary's River and bought close to 30 square miles of land. This land, purchased from the local Native Americans, included the Yeocomico Village, establishing what is now Saint Mary's City.

Prior to the landing of England's colonists and as far back as 3,000 years, several Indian tribes, including the Piscataway-Conoy, Algonquins, and the Susquehannocks called this area home. Evidence of their existence can still be found along the banks of the river in the form of arrowheads, pottery and axe heads.

As the first settlement in Maryland and the fourth permanent English settlement in the New World, this area on the eastern shore was a busy pioneer community. In 1637 Saint Mary's County was established and became known as the "Mother County of Maryland." Saint Mary's County was also the first county to establish peaceful relations with the local Indians and was home to Maryland's first State House.

Today, much of what used to be Saint Mary's City no longer exists. By the time the State House was moved to Annapolis in 1695 and the American Revolution had ended, Lord

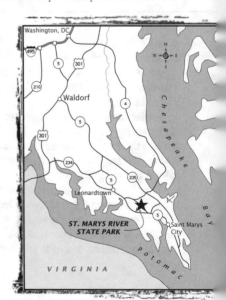

MilesDirections

0.0 START from the parking area and enter at the trailhead (marked by a hiker sign). Immediately after your start, follow the right fork. The left fork will lead you to the same place, but the right one is more fun.
0.18 Turn right at this trail intersection. If you chose the left fork, continue straight.
0.2 Cross a small wooden bridge. Follow the trail to the right.
0.4 Turn left at this intersection and follow the water line toward the dam. If you chose to go left at the previous fork, you will arrive at this intersection 10 yards to your left.
0.45 Cross the dam.
1.0 Turn left on the singletrack. The trailhead is shortly before the road curves up and to the left.
1.6 After a short downhill, cross another small wooden bridge and continue straight. The trail is now blazed white.
2.1 Cross the creek and turn left.
3.0 Bear right at this intersection. The left fork will take you to a small point overlooking the lake—a nice spot for a picnic.

(continues on next page)

Baltimore's capital was gone. However, during the commemoration of Maryland's 300th anniversary in 1934, the original Maryland State House was reconstructed. In 1984, celebrating Maryland's 350th anniversary, other original sites were reconstructed. As time passes, more of Maryland's original buildings and points of interest are identified by more than 150 active archeological excavations which are painstakingly reconstructing history. Today, Saint Mary's City and County are living museums of Maryland's past.

In the 1970s, the state began purchasing land north of Great Mills, named for the mills operating along the banks of the

MilesDirections (continued)

3.4 Bear left and cross another small wooden bridge.

3.5 Continue to the left and over another wooden bridge.

5.1 Cross the creek. The trail continues on the other side. This is a muddy area.

5.3 Locals have built a corduroy bridge over a swampy area.

5.6 Cross yet another small wooden bridge.

5.66 Continue to the left.

7.1 Turn right at this intersection. If you choose to go left, follow the markers in parentheses.

7.2 Turn left then cross the creek. This trail is marked with orange tape.

7.7 Cross a series of small wooden bridges. The trail continues to the left.

8.15 Arrive back at the parking lot.

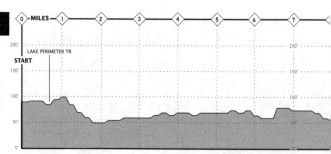

Patuxent River. In 1979 it had completed a dam used to protect the area from spring floods. By 1981, this area was opened to the public, becoming one of Maryland's youngest state parks.

Located on the northern edge of the Saint Mary's River watershed, the park is divided into two sites. Our ride is located on Site 1, which holds the 250-acre Saint Mary's Lake. This area has become a popular freshwater fishing spot and is currently designated as a trophy bass lake. Of more importance to cyclists, Saint Mary's Lake is circled by an 11.5-mile trail, of which eight miles are mapped for your ride. As you pedal through the forest, notice the variety of habitats ranging from wooded acres and grass fields to swamps and streams. Currently, the park is in its early stages of development, so read the main bulletin board for special announcements and information on areas that may be closed to the public.

In Addition...

Maryland Department of Natural Resources:

One of the greatest sources of information for mountain bikers is the Maryland Department of Natural Resources. The majority of Maryland's state parks and forests are open to off-road cycling. A quick phone call will get you all the information you need to make your visits enjoyable and safe. For more information on trails, open areas, and directions to Maryland's state parks and forests call or write one of the following numbers.

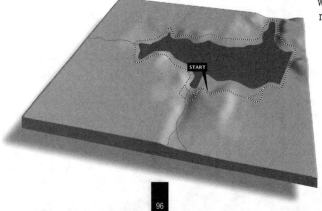

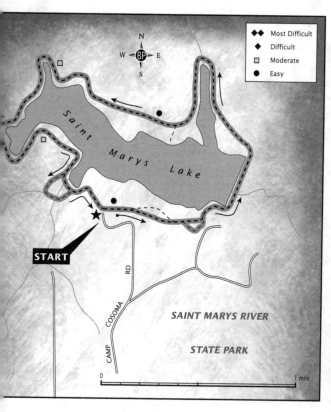

Legend:
- ◆◆ Most Difficult
- ◆ Difficult
- ☐ Moderate
- ● Easy

START

PO RD
COSOMA
CAMP

SAINT MARYS RIVER

STATE PARK

Saint Marys Lake

0 _____ 1 mile

Ride Information

Trail Maintenance Hotline:
Blue Wind Shop (301) 737-2713
Point Lookout State Park
Star Route Box 48
Scotland, MD 20687
(301) 872-5688

Schedule:
Open daily from March 1st through
the third weekend in November:
6 a.m. to sunset

Local Bike Shop:
Blue Wind
9001 Three Notch Road
PO Box 929
California, Maryland 20619
(301) 737-2713
1-800-442-5834

Maps:
USGS maps: Hollywood, MD;
   Solomon Island, MD
DeLorme: Maryland/Delaware Atlas
   and Gazetteer – Page 30 C-3

Maryland Department of Natural Resources
580 Taylor Avenue
Tawes State Office Building
Annapolis, MD 21401
http://gacc.com/dnr/

Cedarville State Forest (Upper Marlboro) 301-888-1410
Deep Creek Lake Recreation Area (Swanton) 301-387-4111
Gambrill State Park (Thurmont) 301-271-7574
Green Ridge State Forest (Flintstone) 301-478-3124
Greenbrier State Park (Boonsboro) 301-791-4767
New Germany State Park (Grantsville) 301-895-5453
Patapsco Valley State Park (Ellicott City) 410-461-5005
Pocomoke River State Park (Snow Hill) 410-632-2566
Rocks State Park (Jarrettsville) 410-557-7994
Seneca Creek State Park (Gaithersburg) 301-924-2282
Susquehanna State Park (Jarrettsville) 410-557-7994
Tuckahoe State Park (Queen Anne) 410-820-1668

Pocomoke State Park

Ride Specs

Start: Nature Center parking lot
Length: 5.5 miles
Rating: Easy to Moderate
Terrain: ORV Trails
Other Uses: Boat launch, boat rental, campfire programs, campsites, fishing, flat water canoeing, hiking trail, playground, swimming, four-wheel drive, motorcross, siteseeing

Getting There

From **Cambridge Maryland** – Take **Route 50** through **Salisbury.** Pick up **Route 12 to Snow Hill, MD.** Once in Snow Hill, turn **left on Market Street (Route 394)** and follow it to **Route 113.** Shortly after Route 394 merges onto Route 113, **turn right into Pocomoke River State Park.** Take your first right and follow the signs to the **Nature Center.**

W elcome to way-down southeastern Maryland in Snow Hill—one of the friendliest areas on Maryland's Eastern Shore. Located in Worcester County along the banks of the Pocomoke River, approximately 3.5 miles south of Snow Hill, are the Pocomoke River State Forest and Park. The Pocomoke River—Native American for "black water"—originates in the Great Cypress Swamp on the Maryland-Delaware border. It then meanders southwesterly for nearly 55 miles through Maryland before flowing into the Pocomoke Sound and the Chesapeake Bay.

English settlers founded historic Snow Hill in 1642—later declared a royal port by William and Mary of England. As such, Snow Hill was the home of a thriving shipbuilding industry, a busy commerce center and, by 1742, home of the Worcester County seat.

The Pocomoke River became a heavily traveled trade route and overnight travel services to Baltimore and Norfolk, Virginia, became regular. Hotels, boarding houses, and a very successful lumber company—the Richardson, Smith and Moore—emerged. For a time, Snow Hill thrived. Then, with the end of the Civil War and the arrival of the railroad and modern transportation, river transportation became outdated. Snow Hill's reign as a successful river city began to wane, its people turning from shipbuilding and commerce to agriculture. Today, Snow Hill remains an historic town and is quietly becoming a popular respite from the big cities to the north. Its proximity to the ocean, the ever-popular Assateague Island, and the scenic Pocomoke River has made Snow Hill a popular vacation destination.

The combination of swamp and upland in this area offers a wide variety of plant and animal life as well. White dogwoods and pink laurels are present throughout the spring months, and visitors may spot playful river otters in the Pocomoke or cast

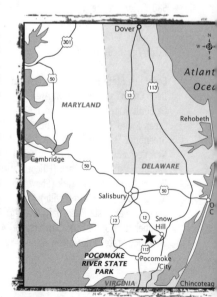

lines out for the more than 50 species of fish. The area has also been described as one of the best environments for bird life along the Atlantic coast. Evidence of this is clear from the 172 species of birds spotted throughout the region, including the Bald Eagle, often seen gliding over the open river.

This ride takes you through 5.5 miles of off road vehicle tracks on the south side of the Pocomoke River through stands of loblolly pine. What this ride lacks in elevation, will be made up by its riding surface. Sections of trail are loose and sandy, making pedaling a chore. Other sections are deep with water and swampy, challenging yet enjoyable to ride. The entire route takes place on a small parcel of land designated for off-road vehicle use. Keep alert, because you may cross paths with a four-wheeler or motorcycle.

As you enter the park, take your first right and park your car by the Nature Center. The trailhead is directly across from the park entrance and clearly marked with a large wooden sign reading "Chandler Trail." This is where the fun begins. The ride takes you through the forest in a counter-clockwise direction along nearly 5.5 miles of ORV tracks. Although your are limited to the off road vehicle tracks, there are several unmarked trails along this ride that are off limits to motorized vehicles. These trails can add mileage to your ride and offer some exciting alternatives to

MilesDirections

0.0 START from the parking area and head back to Route 113. Cross 113. The trailhead is directly across from the park entrance; begin here. Enter the trail marked "Pocomoke River State Forest, Chandler LUV Track."

0.1 Bear right at this intersection.

0.25 Turn left here.

0.57 Turn right on the first road of this three-way intersection.

2.17 Turn left at this intersection.

2.44 Turn right at this intersection.

2.47 Continue straight.

2.8 Continue straight through this and the next intersection.

3.45 Turn left at this intersection. Continue straight.

4.25 Bear left at this intersection.

4.5 Continue straight at this intersection.

4.7 You're back at Route 113. Cross the road and pick up the trail on the other side. Four vertical logs and a "Weapons Prohibited Sign" mark the trail.

5.2 Turn left on the road and bear left at the next intersection.

5.47 Bear to the right and follow the sign to the Nature Center. You're done.

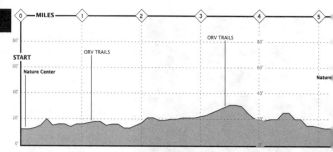

this route. Don't expect any long climbs or speeding descents. This ride is mostly flat and leisurely, providing you a great opportunity to enjoy the beauty of the forest and its wildlife.

Make sure to take some time out to visit nearby Snow Hill and soak in the history of Maryland's past. There are plenty of other activities to do while in the area as well. Flat water canoeing is very popular and gives visitors a chance to experience the Pocomoke River and its Cypress Swamps, this area's biggest attraction. In addition, Assategue Island is only minutes away. This unique spot on the Eastern Shore is home to wild horses, made famous by their annual July swim across the river to Chincoteague. Also in Assategue, is a three-mile "Wildlife Loop" trail restricted to foot and

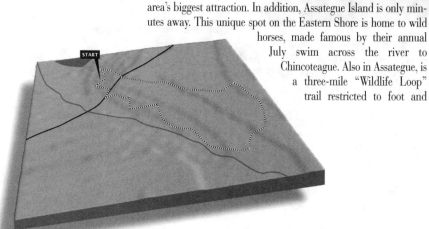

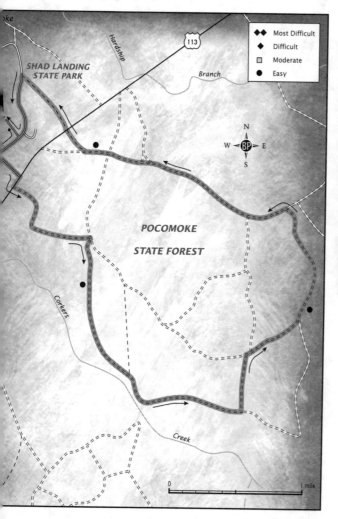

Ride Information

Trail Maintenance Hotline:
Pocomoke River State Forest
3461 Worcester Hwy.
Snow Hill, MD 21863
(410) 632-2566

Schedule:
Open daily from dawn to dusk,
year-round

Maps:
USGS maps: Snow Hill, MD;
  Girdletree, MD/VA
DeLorme: Maryland/Delaware Atlas
  & Gazetteer; Page 30 C-3

bicycle traffic from dawn until 3 p.m.

Although southeastern Maryland is not a mountain biking mecca, there is a wide variety of activities to keep even the hardiest of mountain bikers busy. If you are traveling to the beach and are in dire need of an off-road ride, stop by Snow Hill and the Pocomoke River State Forest. You won't be disappointed.

Old Waterford Dirt Roads

2

Ride Specs

Start: Loudon County High School
Length: 27.5 miles
Rating: Moderate to difficult
Terrain: Rolling dirt/gravel roads

Getting There

From the **Capital Beltway (495)** – Take **Exit 10, Route 7 west (Leesburg Pike)** all the way to **Leesburg** (28 miles). At the Leesburg city limits stay on **BUS Route 7 (Market Street)** through Leesburg. Turn **left on Catoctin Circle**, then, at the **third light, turn left** on **Dry Mill Road. Loudoun County High School** is on your right. Park here.

W hen Amos Janney lead a small group of Quakers in 1733 from Bucks County, Pennsylvania, to the fertile land just west of the Catoctin Mountain along South Fork Creek, he may never have imagined that someday the land he sought would become Virginia's most beautiful horse country, and more significantly for cyclists, the ideal setting for some exceptionally scenic mountain bike rides.

But then again, perhaps he did. Janney and his group of Quakers yearned to be free of the persecutions of the "Old World" and to escape Pennsylvania's ever-increasing population. They sought the solitude and peace that this expansive valley between Catoctin and the Blue Ridge Mountains had to offer. Had this band of Quaker pioneers existed today, it's quite possible that their clothes, while still black cloth, would have been made from skin tight Lycra material made to breathe during a long bicycle ride in the summer heat.

It may be said that Mr. Janney laid the groundwork for mountain biking in this area. Unpaved roads, built since his time, climb along Catoctin Mountain, then roll leisurely along the valley floor. Panoramic views of the green countryside and the mountains beyond are a wonderful backdrop to the horse and dairy farms spread throughout the valley. The Waterford-Hamilton-Leesburg area, just as Amos Janney and his group of settlers discovered, is the perfect location to escape the masses, to be free of the oppressive daily grind of our "New World," and to discover an undisturbed, peaceful haven.

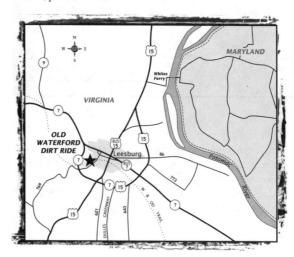

MilesDirections

0.0 START at the Loudoun County High School parking lot off Dry Mill Road. Turn left on Dry Mill Road. Follow the yellow bike route signs (paved).

0.3 Cross over W&OD trail. Continue straight.

0.5 Straight across Loudoun Road.

0.6 Cross Market Street.

0.7 Turn right on Cornwal Street (paved).

0.8 Turn left on Memorial Drive (paved). Memorial Drive stays to the right side of Memorial Hospital, heading toward Gibson Street.

0.9 Turn right on Gibson Street (paved).

1.1 Turn left on Old Waterford Road. Graveyard on the right (paved).

2.3 Old Waterford Road turns to gravel (unpaved).

5.3 Stay right at the intersection with Hurley Lane on Old Waterford Road (unpaved).

7.2 Turn left on Main Water Street (paved). Arrive in the historic town of Waterford.

7.4 Turn left on Old Wheatland Road (paved).

7.7 Old Wheatland Road turns to gravel (unpaved).

10.6 Turn left on Charlestown Pike (VA Route 9) (paved). Be careful along this road. The speed limit for cars is 55 mph.

11.2 Turn right on Hampton Road (unpaved).

(continues on next page)

This route is comprised primarily of unpaved dirt and gravel roads perfect for the off-road tourist looking for more than ballistic singletrack and rugged trails. Stop in the historic town of Waterford and have a look around. Amos Janney settled this little Virginia town and called it Milltown. It was later renamed by a lit-

Miles Directions *(continued)*

11.8 Turn left on Piggott Bottom Road (unpaved).

12.2 Bear left at the stop sign, continuing on Piggott Bottom Road.

14.0 Turn right on Hamilton Station Road (paved).

14.3 Cross W&OD trail.

15.1 Turn right on Colonial Hwy (paved).
Arrive in the historic town of Hamilton.

15.2 Turn left on Harmony Church Road (paved).

15.8 Bear left on Diggs Valley Road (unpaved).

17.2 Diggs Valley Road comes to a 4-way intersection. Turn left, continuing on Diggs Valley Road (unpaved).

17.4 Turn right on Canby Road (unpaved). Stay on Canby all the way to Harmony Church Road.

19.0 Cross Harmony Church Road on Loudon Orchard Road (paved).

(continues on next page)

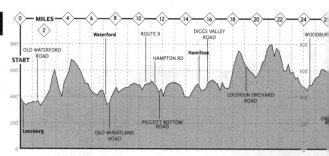

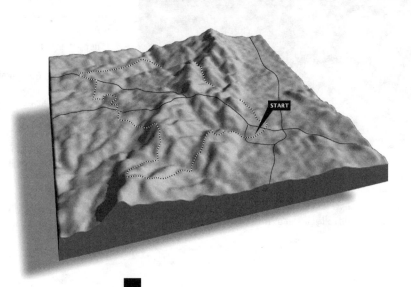

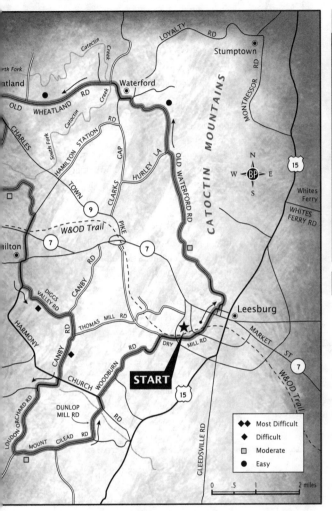

Ride Information

Trail Maintenance Hotline:
None Available

Schedule:
None Available

Maps:
USGS maps: Purcellville, VA;
  Lincoln, VA; Leesburg, VA;
  Waterford, VA
ADC Maps: Loudon County road
  map
DeLorme: Virginia Atlas &
  Gazetteer; Page 79-80 D-1

MilesDirections(continued)

19.7 Bear left, continuing on Loudon Orchard Road (paved).
20.1 Loudoun Orchard turns to gravel (unpaved).
21.4 Turn left on Mount Gilead Road (unpaved).
23.3 Turn left on Dunlop Mill Road (unpaved).
24.1 Turn left on Harmony Church Road (paved).
24.3 Turn right on Woodburn Road (unpaved).
26.7 Turn right on Dry Mill Road.
27.5 Arrive at Loudoun County High School.

tle Irish cobbler whose hometown was Waterford, Ireland. Cross the Washington & Old Dominion Trail into the town of Hamilton for a little break, then be on your way, heading south toward Mount Gilead before riding north again to Leesburg. Be sure to notice the spectacular homes along Loudoun Orchard Road and Mount Gilead Road, and be careful not to bump into the deer residing in force throughout this area.

Ball's Bluff Canal Ride

Ride Specs

Start: Ball's Bluff Battlefield
Length: 31.1 miles
Rating: Difficult due to Catoctin Mountain climb and length of ride
Terrain: Dirt roads, C&O Canal towpath

Getting There

From the **Capital Beltway (495)** – Take **Exit 10, Route 7 west (Leesburg Pike)** all the way to **Leesburg** (28 miles). At the Leesburg city limits, take **Route 15 north** for approximately 1.5 miles, then turn right on **Ball's Bluff Road.** This will take you 0.8 miles to **Ball's Bluff National Cemetery and Battlefield.** Park here and begin your ride.

F ollowing what he believed were instructions from General George McClellan to push south, Union General Stone set in motion a series of events on the night of October 20, 1861, that would result the next evening in carnage on the wooded bluff above the Potomac River.

Reconnaissance reported to General Stone an ill-guarded Confederate camp outside Leesburg, Virginia. Eager for the opportunity to destroy it, Stone positioned his men at Conrad's (Whites) Ferry, Harrisons Island, and Edwards Ferry. Movement across the swollen Potomac began at midnight, but Stone's men found no camp at the reported site. They found, instead, only a moonlit grove of trees, mistaken by his men the previous night as tents.

They chose to continue toward Leesburg and, early that morning, met resistance from a Confederate outpost just north of Leesburg near Ball's Bluff. After hearing of skirmishes with Union soldiers, four companies of Confederate infantry were sent from Leesburg to the previously small outpost just west of Ball's Bluff, pushing the Union troops back toward the river. Throughout the afternoon, a series of advancements and attacks by a continually reinforced Confederate line forced the ill-fated Union troops near the edge of a steep drop to the rocky banks of the Potomac. When Union reinforcement did arrive by climbing a path at the side of the bluff, there was confusion among the officers over who was in command. A decision finally was made to fight their way through Confederate lines, since the only alternative was to retreat off the bluff, 90 feet down to the river below. But just as the Union troops

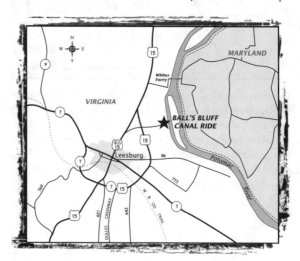

MilesDirections

0.0 START at Ball's Bluff National Battlefield Park. Follow Ball's Bluff Road to Route 15 (Leesburg Pike).

1.0 Turn right on Route 15 North (Leesburg Pike)—ride on the shoulder.

4.1 Turn left on Montressor Road (Route 661)—(unpaved).

5.0 Bear right, continuing on Montressor Road.

7.2 Turn right on Stumptown Road (Route 662)—(paved).

7.7 Turn left on New Valley Church Road Route 663)—(paved).

8.2 Turn right on Taylorstown Road Route 663)—(paved).

9.9 Taylorstown Road turns to gravel and begins a steep ascent (unpaved).

10.7 Reach the summit of this climb. Begin a fast, gravelly descent.

11.3 Turn right on Furnace Mountain Road (Route 665) at the bottom of the descent (unpaved). Food 0.2 miles ahead on Taylorstown Road.

13.7 Turn right on Lovettsville Road (Route 672)—(paved).

13.75 Turn left on Route 15 North and cross the bridge over the Potomac. (Use the sidewalk across the bridge.)

(continues on next page)

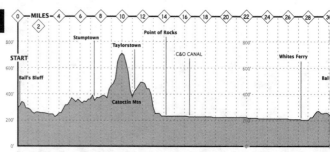

MilesDirections (continued)

14.3 Once across the bridge, turn right on Route 28 (paved) into Point of Rocks, MD. There's a general store one block up the road. Turn right immediately on Commerce Street (this is a small street that goes behind the houses on Main Street). Follow this across the railroad track, then over the wooden bridge to the C&O Canal towpath (paved).

14.4 Turn left on the C&O Canal towpath, heading down river (unpaved).

27.1 Turn right on Whites Ferry Road to Whites Ferry (paved).

Take the ferry across the Potomac. Remember to have the toll with you. 50¢ for bicycles.

28.4 Turn left on Route 15 South (James Monroe Highway)— (paved—ride on the shoulder).

30.1 Turn left on Ball's Bluff Road toward the battlefield (paved).

31.1 Arrive back at Ball's Bluff National Battlefield.

attempted their advance, Confederates launched a murderous attack, blocking both the path that Union reinforcements had previously climbed and any chance for their retreat. Federal troops were suddenly forced to choose between furious Confederate gunfire and a suicidal leap to the rocks far below. Nearly 1,000 Union soldiers were lost that afternoon, dealing a severe blow to the Northern army, which was still reeling from its recent defeat at the first Battle of Bull Run. Ball's Bluff National Cemetery and Battlefield, the country's smallest national battlefield, remains today a quiet testimony to America's most violent era.

This ride, which begins at Ball's Bluff, offers a real variation in terrain to cyclists. Traveling first in Virginia, the course alternates between paved and unpaved roads, starting out flat, then rolling, before getting very hilly as it crosses over Catoctin Mountain. On the Maryland side, you can relax along the all-flat, all-dirt C&O Canal towpath that meanders along the scenic Potomac River. Along the way, you will cross over the Monocacy Aqueduct, the largest aqueduct along the 185-mile canal. Catch the ferry at Whites Ferry to cross back over to the Virginia side, then return to the start of the ride.

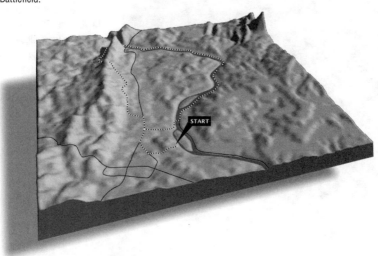

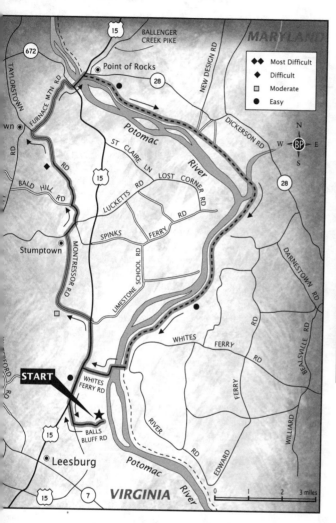

Most Difficult ◆◆
Difficult ◆
Moderate □
Easy ●

Ride Information

Trail Maintenance Hotline:
C&O Canal headquarters:
(301) 739-4200

Costs:
Whites Ferry: 50¢ for bicycles, $2
for cars

Schedule:
Ball's Bluff National Cemetery is
open from dawn to dusk.
Whites Ferry is open from 6 a.m.
to 11 p.m. every day.

Maps:
USGS maps: Leesburg, VA;
    Waterford, VA; Point of Rocks,
    MD; Poolesville, MD.
ADC Maps: Loudon County, VA;
    Montgomery County, MD
DeLorme: Virginia Atlas &
    Gazetteer; Page 80 C-1

Middleburg Vineyards Tour

Ride Specs

Start: Middleburg Elementary School
Length: 23.1 miles
Rating: Moderate to Difficult (due to length)
Terrain: Mostly easy rolling, unpaved dirt and gravel roads

Getting There

From the **Capital Beltway (495)** – Take **I-66 west** 8.5 miles to **Exit 57, Route 50 west**. Go 23 miles on Route 50 west into **Middleburg.** John Mosby Highway (Route 50) becomes **Washington Street** within Middleburg town limits. From Washington Street, turn **right** on **Route 626, Madison Street.** Go 0.1 miles and **turn right** into the **Middleburg Elementary School** parking lot.

A h, wine! To sip the fruit is lots of fun, but to ride and drink can't be outdone.

Yes, this ride travels through some of Virginia's finest wine country, where visits to the vineyards are always welcome and wine tasting is just part of the tour.

You start in the historic town of Middleburg, a small, touristy outpost in the middle of Hunt Country. Horses abound in this magnificent countryside. A town with a rich history, Middleburg has enjoyed its share of good fortune. Established in 1787, this centuries-old town was even graced by a U.S. president when the Kennedy family attended the local Catholic church and built a home just outside town.

The ride starts on a route toward Piedmont Vineyard but breaks off from the main road onto backcountry dirt, perfect for an off-road tourist. This first section rolls comfortably past small estates and low-key horse farms. But when you turn east, the roads lift you into the hills. You'll pass some of the old and new—abandoned stone houses and state-of-the-art homes—then head toward Meredyth Vineyard to lavish in the land of the well-to-do. Gorgeous estates rest on acres of open land, where thoroughbreds graze in the warm sun. What a wonderful place to ride and dream. But don't forget to stop at the vineyard. (Their hours are from 10-4 p.m.) The rest of the ride rolls up and down below Bull Run Mountain, taking you past one more vineyard, the Swedenburg Estate, before leading you back into Middleburg.

If the wine doesn't get the best of you, then enjoy the endless dirt roads scattered throughout this region. This is excellent off-road riding for cyclists looking for a change.

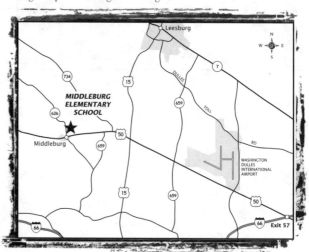

Mountain Biking and Wine.

If my assumption is correct, many of you are like myself and may have never really refined your tastes with good wine. After all, we're mountain bikers for heaven's sake! If such is the case, then you may also find yourselves feeling about as silly and uneducated as I have when the proprietor of a winery serves samples of the vineyard's great variety of wines. You may understand little to none about what this person is talking about, and if you're like me, you might politely sip the wine, nod your head at each flavor's description, and wonder how they can arrive at so many names for such similar tastes. Hopefully, after reading some of the following information before cycling up to a vineyard's door, you may quite miraculously understand some of what the proprietor is telling you about their latest flavors and wines and enjoy the free samples that much more. Just remember, the best way to learn about wines is to drink them.

Wine is the fermented juice of grapes. Nearly all the wine made throughout the world comes from one species of grape—Vitis vinifera. As many as 4,000 varieties of grape have been developed from this one species, each of which differs, sometimes only slightly, from each other in size, color, shape of the berry, juice composition, ripening time, and resistance to disease. Only about a dozen of the 4,000 or more varieties of grapes are commonly used for winemaking around the world. Chiefs among them are: Chardonnay, Riesling, Cabernet Sauvignon, Sauvignon Blanc, Pinot Noir, Gewürztraminer, and Muscat.

The main reason the varieties of Vitis vinifera are used throughout the world in wine production is for their high sugar content when ripe. Wine with an alcohol content of 10 percent or slightly higher is produced from the grapes' natural sugar content after fermentation. Wines with less alcohol are unstable and subject to bacterial spoilage.

Wine Colors

We're all familiar with colors of wine: white wine, rosé, and red wine. But why the different colors and what's the big deal anyway?

MilesDirections

0.0 START at the Middleburg Elementary School parking lot. Turn left on Route 626, Madison Street (paved).

0.1 Turn right on Washington Street (Route 50)—(paved).

0.3 Turn left on Plains Road (Route 626). Follow the purple vineyard sign (paved).

1.1 Turn right on Route 705 (paved).

1.2 Route 705 changes to dirt (unpaved).

3.2 Stay straight on Route 705 at this intersection. Route 706 turns right.

3.4 Stay right on Route 705 at this intersection. Route 706 turns left.

4.2 Turn left at the "T," continuing on Route 705. Route 708 goes right (unpaved).

5.3 Turn left at the stop sign on Route 702 (unpaved).

7.6 Turn left on Route 626 (paved).

7.9 Bear right on Route 679 at the bottom of the descent. This turns into Route 628.

9.1 Turn left on Route 628. This is slightly hidden. The turn comes after a long rock wall on the left, just past a large brick house with three chimneys (unpaved).

9.4 Meredyth Vineyards on the left. Stop in for a tour. Hours are from 10 a.m. to 4 p.m.

(continues on next page)

MilesDirections (continued)

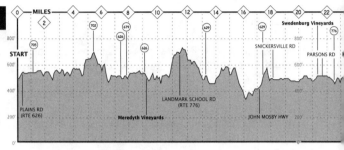

11.5 Turn right on Landmark School Road (Route 776)—(paved).

For those who have had enough, you can turn left on Landmark School Road and take the shortcut back to Middleburg—2.4 miles.

13.2 Turn left on Champe Road (Route 629)—(unpaved).

17.1 Turn left on John Mosby Highway (Route 50). Be careful of traffic (paved).

17.5 Turn right on Cobb House Road (Route 629)—(unpaved)

18.5 Turn left on Snickersville Road (paved).

18.8 Turn left at the bottom of the hill on Carters Farm Road (Route 627)—(unpaved).

21.3 Turn right on John Mosby Highway (Route 50)—(paved). Pass Swedenburg Estate Vineyard. Stop for a sip of wine before continuing on.

21.5 Turn left on Parsons Road (Route 627)—(unpaved).

(continues on next page)

• **White wine** is produced when only the juice from the grape is used. The skin is removed before fermentation begins. The juice is normally colorless, though some varieties have a pink to reddish color. Because only the grape's juice is used, white wine tends to be much lighter, thus much easier to the palette for most people unfamiliar with drinking wine.

• **A rosé** or **blush** is produced when the skins of red or black grapes are removed after fermentation has begun.

• **Red wine** is produced when whole, crushed red or black grapes are used, including the skins. Red wine has a significantly more robust flavor than white wine.

What are we supposed to eat with this stuff with anyway?

In general, it's suggested that we drink white wines with light foods such as salads, chicken, and fish. Red wines are recommended for heavier flavored foods such as beef, lamb, and sometimes pork. The reasons are strictly for the palette. A strong tasting red wine may overwhelm the light flavors of chicken or fish, while the lighter and sometimes sweeter flavor of white wine may get lost on a hearty, juicy steak. What should cyclists drink with their spaghetti? Either one is fine. Heck, who cares? It's wine!

Where does it come from?

Although Italy produces more wine, the world's leading wine producer in terms of quality is France, with outstanding products from Bordeaux and Burgundy, the Loire and Rhone valleys, and Alsace. Other major producers are Spain, the US, Germany, Chile, Argentina, South Africa, and Australia. In the US, California is the leading wine-producing region. Central Virginia is a close second.

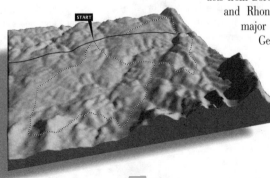

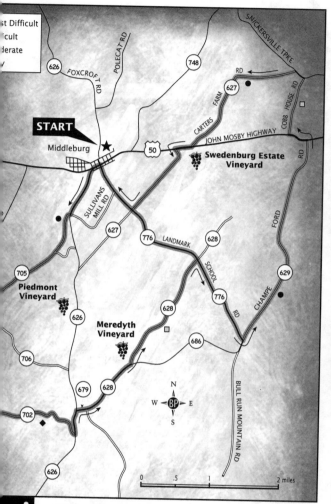

Ride Information

Wine Tasting Hotline:
Meredyth Vineyard:
(540) 687-6277
Piedmont Vineyard:
(540) 687-5528
Swedenburg Estate Vineyard
(540) 687-5219

Schedule:
Meredyth Vineyard:
10-5, 7 days a week-N/C
Piedmont Vineyard:
10-4, 7 days a week-N/C
Swedenburg Estate Vineyard
10-4, 7 days a week-N/C

Maps:
USGS maps: Rectortown, VA;
   Middleburg, VA
ADC Maps: Loudon County road
   map, Fauquier County road map
DeLorme: Virginia Atlas &
   Gazetteer; Page 75 A-7

MilesDirections (continued)

22.6 Turn right on Landmark School Road (Route 776)— (paved).
23.0 Arrive back in Middleburg. Cross Washington Street to Madison Street.
23.1 Turn right into the school parking lot. Drink too much wine?

In Addition...

White wine: Red and white grapes are stemmed and crushed before going into a horizontal press for more crushing (end plates in the horizontal press move toward each other and crush the grapes). The juice (sans the skin) then flows to a vat for fermenting. The juice has not had time to pick up color from the skins, leaving it white.

Red and **rosé wines:** The crushed grapes go directly into fermenting vats with their skins. After fermenting, the unpalatable red press wine is mixed with free-run wine. The dry skins and pulp (called marc) can be distilled into cheap brandy.

Fermentation starts when wine yeasts on the skins of ripe grapes come in contact with the grape juice. After running off into casks, the new wine then undergoes a series of chemical processes, including oxidation, precipitation of proteins, and fermentation of chemical compounds. Each of these processes creates the wine's characteristic bouquet (aroma). After periodic clarification and aging in casks, the wine is ready to be bottled.

Great Falls National Park

Ride Specs

Start: Visitors Center
Length: 6.8 miles
Rating: Moderate
Terrain: Rocky, dirt trails; fire roads
Other Uses: Hiking, horseback riding, climbing, kayaking, site seeing

Getting There

From the **Capital Beltway (495)** – From Exit-13 northwest of McLean, take **Route 193 (Georgetown Pike)** west toward Great Falls. Go about four miles, then turn **right** on **Old Dominion Drive.** Go one mile to the end of the park entrance road and park at the **Visitors Center.** Telephones, water, food, toilet, and information available.

Great Falls is one of the United State's most popular national parks. How appropriate then for it to be located just 14 miles from our nation's capital. And what a thrill for cyclists to know that mountain biking is not only allowed at the park—it's welcomed.

Along with hikers, historians, rock climbers, and kayakers, off-road cyclists come in droves to enjoy Great Falls' public resources. There are over five miles of designated trails to enjoy in this park, all of which conveniently intersect to create hours of off-road adventure. The trails vary in intensity, ranging from rolling forest roads beneath tall oaks and maples to steep, rocky singletrack, overlooking the dramatic Mather Gorge. The park's unequaled beauty, proximity to Washington, and accessible trails combine to make Great Falls National Park Northern Virginia's most popular off-road cycling haven.

The ride begins at the Visitors Center parking lot and travels south along Old Carriage Road through the middle of the park.

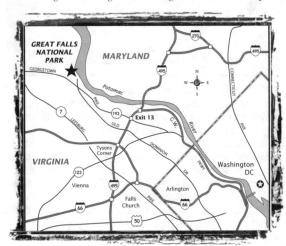

Old Carriage was used in the 1700s to carry settlers to their dwellings at Matildaville, ruins of which still stand today. Henry Lee, a Revolutionary War hero and friend of George Washington's developed this small town. Named after Lee's first wife, Matildaville lasted only three decades before fading into history.

The route bends deep into the park and travels up and down the rocky pass along Ridge Trail. During the winter months, breathtaking views of the gorge show through deciduous trees. The trail then descends quickly to the Potomac (another great view) and follows along Difficult Run before heading north again back toward the start.

Great Falls has always been a popular place to visit for locals and world tourists alike. Some have come to survey the river's rapids, including George Washington, who formed the Patowmack Company in 1784 to build a series of canals around the falls. Theodore Roosevelt would come to Great Falls to hike and ride horses during his presidency. Today, thousands come to enjoy Great Falls as well. But they don't come to build canals, develop towns, make trade, or seek solitude from the presidential office. They come only to ride the Park's great trails and witness the magnificent scenery at Great Falls National Park.

MilesDirections

0.0 START at Great Falls Visitors Center. Follow the Horse/Biker trail south along Entrance Road.

0.4 Bear right at the restrooms and go around the steel gate on Old Carriage Road (unpaved).

1.1 Bear left down the trail to Sandy Landing.

1.3 Arrive at Sandy Landing. A beautiful spot along the river, great for viewing Mather Gorge. Return to Old Carriage Road.

1.5 Turn left, continuing on Old Carriage Road. Begin a steady uphill.

1.9 Turn left near the top of this climb on Ridge Trail.

2.7 Turn left after the steep descent on Difficult Run Trail. Head toward the Potomac.

2.9 Arrive at the Potomac River. This is another great spot to view Sherwin Island where Mather Gorge and the Potomac River merge. Turn around and follow Difficult Run Trail west along Difficult Run Creek toward Georgetown Pike.

3.6 Turn right on Georgetown Pike. Be careful with traffic and ride on the dirt shoulder.

3.8 Turn right on Old Carriage Road. This is the first dirt road you come to along Georgetown Pike. Go around the gate and begin climbing.

4.0 Turn left on Ridge Trail. Follow this toward the entrance road.

(continues on next page)

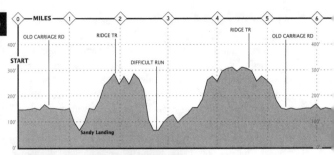

MilesDirections *(continued)*

4.7 Reach Great Falls National Park's entrance road (Old Dominion Road). Turn around and continue back on Ridge Trail.
5.4 Turn left on Old Carriage Road.
6.4 Go through the gate at the beginning of Old Carriage Road and head back to the parking lot at the Visitors Center.
6.8 Arrive back at the Visitors Center and parking lot.

In Addition...

Information, information, information...

One of the major fuels of trade in our nation's capital is information. It is the business of Washington. And the government is the major source and collector of this valuable resource in today's information age. The following excerpt from Compton's Interactive Encyclopedia attributes to the explosive value placed on information and what it has meant to Washington's economy.

"Since the computer revolution of the 1970s, the services sector has become an increasingly important industry in the city. With more information to transmit and record, the publishing, broadcasting, and video industries have flourished. A world telecommunications center, Washington is the base of more than 12,000 journalists who report news primarily about the government. Every major news publication in the world maintains its own Washington bureau of correspondents.

The oldest local daily newspaper is the influential Washington Post, which was found-

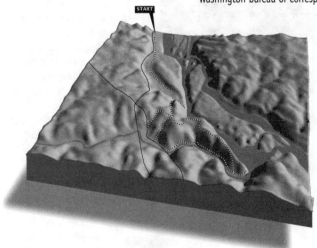

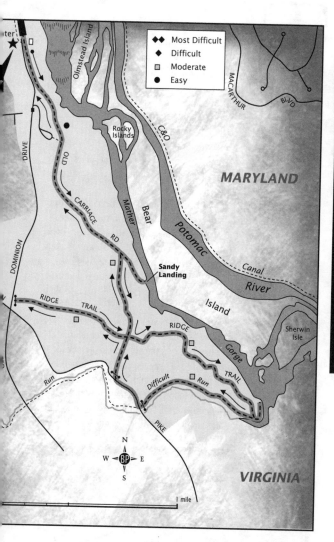

Ride Information

Trail Maintenance Hotline:
National Park Service
(703) 759-2915

Costs:
$2 entrance fee is charged

Schedule:
Park is open from 7 a.m.
to sunset

Maps:
USGS maps: Vienna, VA; Falls
    Church, VA
ADC Maps: Northern Virginia road
    map
DeLorme: Virginia Atlas &
    Gazetteer; Page 76 A-4
National Park Service Official Trail
    Map and Guide

ed in 1877. In 1982 the Rev. Sun Myung Moon's Unification church began publishing the Washington Times on weekdays. The nationally distributed USA Today was also launched from Washington that year. Already the home of the world's largest publisher, the Government Printing Office, Washington has begun to house tradebook publishing firms."

Compton's NewMedia, Inc.

Difficult Run

Ride Specs

Start: Twin Branches Nature Trail
Length: 24 miles round trip
Rating: Moderate
Terrain: Singletrack trails/bike path
Other Uses: Hiking, horseback riding

Getting There

From the **Capital Beltway (495)** – Take the **Washington-Dulles Access Road** (toll road) west for 7 miles to **Exit 5, Hunter Mill Road.** Go **south** on Hunter Mill Road to **Sunrise Valley Road** and **turn right.** Go half a mile and **turn left** on **South Lakes Drive.** Turn **left** on **Twin Branches Road**. Follow Twin Branches Road to **Glade Drive** and park. **Twin Branches Trail** starts here.

This 12-mile route from Reston, Virginia, to Great Falls National Park may define what is becoming a new kind of trailway through growing suburban landscapes. Combining a mixture of clay-surfaced singletrack, bike paths, public parkland, and creek corridors, this ride follows what is perhaps the longest and most unique trail system in the Washington/Baltimore region.

The first half of the ride weaves its way through Reston, Virginia, once a leader in community planning. One of the unique features setting this small city apart is its intricate network of public walkways, designed to lead you anywhere you want to go without having to get on the roads.

The ride begins at the trailhead for Twin Branches Nature Trail on Twin Branches Road and heads east toward the Potomac. Should you be interested in exploring Glade Stream Valley Park, simply head west at this starting point and ride downhill along the paved path. This path will lead you alongside the Glade, a trickling creek at the southern edge of the Reston development. You can choose to ride on a natural-surface trail or an asphalt path, both of which parallel the creek for three miles to Colts Neck Road. Along the Glade, visitors are treated to preserved natural habitats and a bounty of whistling feathered companions.

Start your ride and head east on the all-dirt singletrack along Twin Branches Nature Trail. This rugged trail system will lead you all the way to the Washington & Old Dominion Bike Trail. Turn left on the W&OD and follow it for a few miles to Michael Faraday Court, where another trail, beginning at the end of the court, takes you winding along Colvin Run through Lake Fairfax

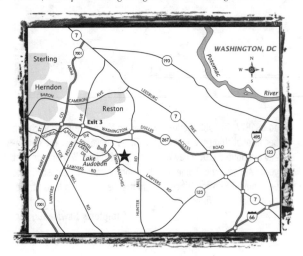

MilesDirections

0.0 START from the Twin Branches Nature Trail trailhead on the east side of Twin Branches Road. The trailhead on the west side of the road takes you along Glade Trail. From the trailhead, split left, following Twin Branches Nature Trail downhill into the woods.

0.8 Twin Branches Nature Trail comes to a "T" just after crossing a small wooden bridge. Turn left toward the W&OD Bike Trail. Turning right leads you into private property.

0.9 Turn left on the W&OD Bike Trail.

2.0 Cross Sunrise Valley Drive.

2.3 Go underneath Dulles Access Road.

2.6 Cross Sunset Hills Road.

2.9 Turn right into Michael Faraday Court. Go to the end of the court and look for a small dirt trail leading up a little grassy hill into Reston Industrial Park. Bear left through this park on Colvin Run Trail, marked by a wooden post with a white band and a horseshoe on it. This trail descends rapidly to Colvin Run.

3.8 Colvin Run Trail crosses over a little creek and comes to "T." Turn left at this split, following the Lake Fairfax Nature Trail up to the camping grounds and playing fields of Lake Fairfax.

4.3 Turn right up the gravel road to the playing fields. Playing fields on the right, group camping on the left. Follow the gravel road to Lake Fairfax Dam.

(continues on next page)

MilesDirections *(continued)*

4.7 Cross Lake Fairfax Dam into the main park area. Food, drinks, bathrooms, working train, and park office. Take a break for lunch if you wish. Follow the horse trail, beginning in front of the park office, down the hill south of the dam and back toward Colvin Run.

5.5 Cross Hunter Mill Road. Follow the marked horse trail (white blaze with horseshoe) along Colvin Run. This trail takes you all the way to Great Falls National Park.

6.7 Turn left on Carpers Farm Way to the light at Leesburg Pike (Route 7). Cross Leesburg Pike, then immediately turn right, following this unimproved road to the end.

NOTE

You must cross Difficult Run a number of times along this last section of trail. The creek is wide virtually guaranteeing a wet ride.

Continuing from Leesburg Pike to Great Falls.

6.9 Follow the horse trail (white blaze) at the end of this road into the woods. This leads you along Difficult Run toward the Potomac.

7.5 Cross Difficult Run. The trail continues on the other side of the creek.

(continues on next page)

Park. You may wish to stop for lunch at this 479-acre park and enjoy the beautiful lake, take a train ride, or even go for a swim. Down the hill to the southeast side of the park, the trail resumes its course along Colvin Run, well marked for horseback riding. It then continues east, across Leesburg Pike to Difficult Run. The trail comes to a scenic end at the Potomac River in Great Falls National Park, where you can watch the turbulent water rushing through Mather Gorge.

Please be aware of the rapidly deteriorating conditions of the trailway along Difficult Run. In recent years, this scenic, wooded path, tracing the **banks** of the creek, has been deformed into a muddy bog, slogging its way along a course of disaster for anyone hoping to use this creek corridor in the future. Be very delicate on this trail, and ride only when the ground is dry. Your help in preserving this trail will stand to benefit everyone in years to come. Contact the Fairfax County or National Park Service to help maintain the trail, then gather a group of friends together on a Saturday afternoon and, with park-service guidance, put some sweat back into the trail.

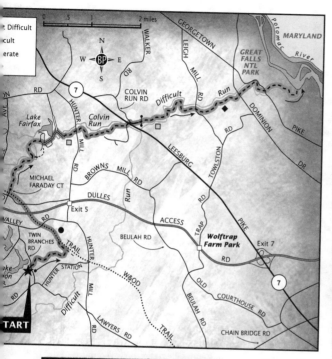

Ride Information

Trail Maintenance Hotline:
Fairfax County Park Service:
(703) 246-5741
National Park Service:
(703) 759-2915
Reston Association (The Glade):
(703) 437-7658

Schedule:
Parks and trails open from dawn
until dusk year-round

Maps:
USGS maps: Vienna, VA; Falls
    Church, VA
ADC maps: Northern Virginia road
    map;
DeLorme: Virginia Atlas &
    Gazetteer: Page 76 A-3
Lake Fairfax Park and trail map;
Great Falls map and trail guide

In Addition...

HELP!

The trail along Difficult Creek to Great Falls is in great need of attention. In order for it to remain open to public use, it must be treated delicately. You will encounter a great deal of mud and trail erosion, so use your best judgement before proceeding the rest of the way to the Potomac.

• Avoid riding here when the ground may be wet, especially after a rainstorm or during the spring thawing season.

• Always stay on the trail. It's better to walk your bike through the muddy sections than to ride around them, thus widening the trail even further.

• Contact the Fairfax County Parks Service or the National Park Service and get involved to repair and maintain this very unique off-road trail. It is the only trail connecting the Northern Virginia suburbs with the Potomac River and Great Falls.

MilesDirections (continued)

8.5 Cross Leigh Mill Road. Continue straight on Difficult Run Trail. Equestrian park on the right.
10.2 Cross at the low point in the creek from the right side of Difficult Run to the left side. The trail along the right side of the creek ends.
10.6 Go underneath Old Dominion Road. Enter Great Falls National Park.
10.8 Cross Difficult Run again. Smooth concrete layers the creek bottom here. Be careful crossing.
11.0 Cross Difficult Run.
11.2 Cross Difficult Run one last time. Follow Difficult Run to the right, going underneath Georgetown Pike. This continues to the Potomac River.
12.0 Reach the Potomac River at the southern end of Mather Gorge.

Centreville Power Lines

2

Centreville had been trying to grow for some time — but for a while was having an altogether tough time of it. Since its establishment in 1792, this small trading center, located nearly equidistant from Leesburg, Warrenton, Middleburg, Washington, Georgetown, and Alexandria, had tried diligently to become more than just a rest stop along Braddock Road.

When construction began on Little River Turnpike in the late eighteenth century, for example, the town hoped this trade highway, stretching west from Alexandria, would be built to pass through their community. Alexandria was, at the time, the Potomac's largest market town. Developers, however, routed Little River Turnpike north in favor of smoother, more even terrain, bypassing the town altogether. The town later tried to house the District Court of Virginia, which served Fairfax, Fauquier, Loudoun, and Prince William Counties. This idea was also rejected in favor of Dumfries in Prince William County. Ever persistent, Centreville founded what it hoped would become a prestigious academy to attract outside scholars to take up residence in local homes. This also went without much success. At one time, Centreville was even known as a local center for slave rental and trade. But into the twentieth century, this small town remained nothing more than the unimposing rest stop it had always been.

As you pass through Centreville today, however, much of this history may seem distant and unfamiliar, because the town has suddenly become a sprawling community of subdivisions, shopping centers, and beltway commuters. And it continues to expand at a phenomenal rate further and further west.

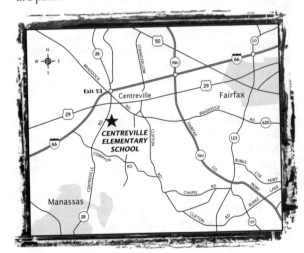

MilesDirections

0.0 START at Centreville Elementary School. Travel south along the asphalt path parallel to Centreville Road. This leads you directly to the power lines.

0.2 Turn left off the asphalt path and hit the dirt trails beneath the power lines. Follow the trail on the left side.

0.75 Cross Bay Valley Lane.

0.8 Turn left at the small fenced-in substation, following the secondary power lines that run north along Little Rocky Run Creek to Braddock Road.

2.0 Pass a small park with tennis courts.

2.2 Re-enter the trail on the right side of the power lines, after passing the park.

2.4 Climb up the embankment at Braddock Road and turn right on the asphalt path. At this point, the trail beneath the power lines disappears as the power lines parallel Braddock Road.

2.8 Turn right on the asphalt bike path along Union Mill Road.

3.1 Centreville High School on the left.

4.3 Bike path ends. Continue riding along the shoulder. Be careful of traffic.

(continues on next page)

MilesDirections *(continued)*

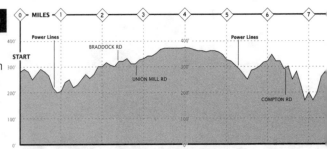

4.8 At this intersection with Compton Road, go straight through the stop sign, continuing on Union Mill Road. Union Mill Road continues into a new housing development. Follow this to the power lines.

5.3 Turn right off Union Mill Road and ride to the power lines, heading west back to Centreville Road.

6.4 Cross Compton Road.

7.0 Pass the small fenced-in power station on the right. Continue straight. Cross Bay Valley Lane.

7.7 Reach Centreville Road. Turn right on the asphalt bike path back toward the school.

7.8 Arrive back at Centreville Elementary School. Tough ride!

Centreville is not unlike many communities surrounding the Washington/Baltimore area that have, in the last 10 to 20 years, seen tremendous growth. This explosive growth has, in most cases, virtually wiped out the small-town flavor that dominated the region west of the cities. Towns and villages, desperate for so long to attract more people and new businesses, could never have anticipated the recent boom in development, which has turned these small hamlets into huge bedroom communities for the Washington/Baltimore megalopolis.

With this growth, precious back roads and trails were permanently lost, forcing cyclists to look even harder for new places to ride. Thus, the discovery of the power lines! They may not be scenic mountain roads with heavenly vistas, but the rugged trails beneath these crackling wires make for the ultimate off-road adventure. They have it all—

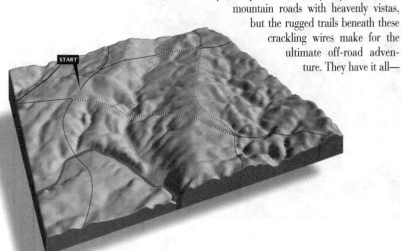

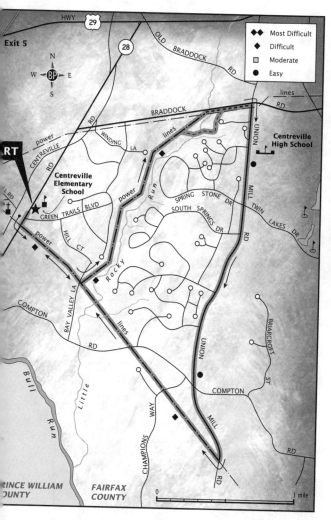

Ride Information

Trail Maintenance Hotline:
None available

Schedule:
None available

Maps:
USGS maps: Manassas, VA
ADC Maps: Northern Virginia Road Map
DeLorme: Virginia Atlas & Gazetteer; Page 76 B-2

rocks, ditches, hills, dirt, and most importantly, open land on which to ride. You'll find yourself crashing down rocky descents, slogging through muddy streambeds, then up and over steep, rutted climbs that snake back and forth beneath the super-charged black cables.

The most important thing to remember when riding the power lines is there is always a way through the obstacles. Sometimes you just have to find it. Have fun!

South Run Power Lines

2

Start: South Run Park
Length: 10.1 miles
Rating: Difficult
Terrain: Hilly singletrack/ pavement

Many of you may never have considered that the electric company would have anything to do with some of the most challenging and rugged mountain biking terrain anywhere. As this and the previous ride reveal, however, off-road cycling just doesn't get any better than this.

They zap and crackle nearly 60 feet above you, and you wonder just how many volts are rushing at light speed through those high-voltage wires. But is this of any consequence when you have miles of twisting, rugged trails through what resembles a linear wasteland?

Power lines—ideal bike lanes (for a mountain bike) exist everywhere. Electric companies have often permitted and even encouraged the use of their land beneath these high-voltage giants for such things as linear parks, equestrian trails, and hiker-biker paths (i.e. sections of the Washington & Old Dominion Trail). However, not all land beneath the power lines is accessible to the public, and this must be understood.

All the power lines you see stretch over private property, whether owned by the power company themselves or individual landowners. In many cases, these lines cross property where trespassing is taken very seriously. Do not ride through these areas! Fortunately, it's usually easy to tell what areas are strictly off-limits. For example, when power lines cross a farmer's soybean field or over someone's backyard, this land is not a place to ride your bike. It's also easy to recognize whether the trail is fit for riding. Not all land beneath the power lines is maintained for easy access, and often this land becomes so overgrown with thorny weeds and

Getting There

From the **Capital Beltway (495)** – take **I-95 south toward Richmond.** Go only about 0.5 miles and take **Springfield Exit 57, Route 644 west (Old Keene Mill Road).** Follow Old Keene Mill Road west 3 miles, then turn **left** on **Huntsman Blvd.** Follow Huntsman Blvd 1.5 miles to **Fairfax County Parkway**. Turn **right** on the parkway and go about 0.3 miles. Turn **left** into **South Run District Park.** Parking, water, phones, toilets, and showers are available.

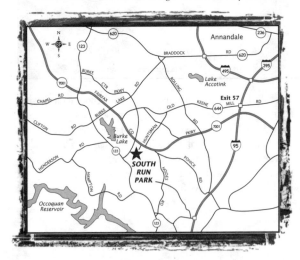

MilesDirections

0.0 START at the South Run Recreation Center, behind the main building and field house. Follow the paved path from the rear parking area down into the woods.

0.2 At the bottom of the hill, follow the asphalt path to the right along South Run.

0.4 Reach the power lines. Turn left, cross South Run stream, and travel south along the dirt trail beneath the power lines.

0.8 The power lines cross Chapel Oak Court and Oak Bridge Place. Follow this to Ox Road. Cross Route 123 (Ox Road) and continue on the power lines.

1.2 Cross the gas pipeline. Continue straight.

2.0 Continue passed the enormous power station on your left.

2.7 Turn right on Hampton Road toward Fountainhead Park (paved).

4.9 Reach Fountainhead Park entrance. Turn left to go down to the marina and concessions building if you'd like.

FOOD. 0.8 miles to the marina and concession stand. There is a network of wooded hiking trails within Fountainhead Park. These trails go all the way up to Bull Run Park.

6.3 Turn right on Henderson Road.

7.1 At the intersection of Henderson Road and Windermere Lane, turn off the road by the brick English Hills subdivision sign, and hop on the equestrian trail paralleling the right side of Henderson Road. This trail goes all the way to Route 123 (Ox Road).

razor-sharp sawgrass that riding would be more a blood bath than a good time. Some land, though, is just right for a challenging and exciting off-road experience. These places have few, if any, points of contention in regard to trespassing. And the terrain, while resembling something from a Mad Max movie, has negotiable singletrack or jeep trails from which you can emerge unscathed by the vicious prickers.

The two rides in this book are of the latter type of power-line

(continues on next page)

MilesDirections *(continued)*

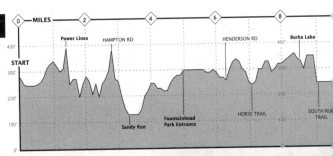

8.3 Cross Route 123 (Ox Road) on the Singletrack Trail directly across from Henderson Road. (Look just inches to the right of the yellow directional sign. The trail begins here). Be very careful crossing Route 123. The traffic is often very heavy.

8.4 Bear right at the fork in the trail.

8.6 Arrive at Burke Lake Dam. Turn right, traveling across the dam.

8.8 Once across the dam, turn right on the asphalt trail leading you away from the lake. This takes you back to South Run Park. (You could turn left and follow this dirt path all the way around the lake. Approximately five miles around.)

9.7 Cross underneath Lee Chapel Road.

9.9 Cross the power lines. Continue straight along the asphalt path.

10.1 Arrive back at South Run Park.

riding, and both offer a tremendous challenge to any singletrack junky. It's important also to realize that on these rides there is always a way forward. Part of the challenge along these rugged trails is the constant presence of obstacles, whether it be rocks, logs, stream crossings, or thick mud. This is nothing but good, clean fun for those into this type of challenge.

This ride follows the power lines south from South Run Park to Hampton Road. Although you must travel pavement along the second part of this ride, traffic is light and scenery fantastic. Zoning in this area is five acres minimum, so houses and lots tend to be both beautiful and enormous. Hampton winds its way along the wooded lane alongside

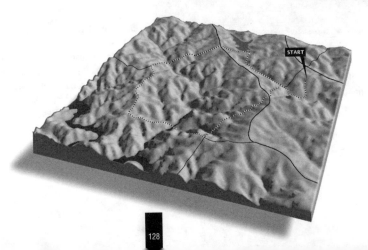

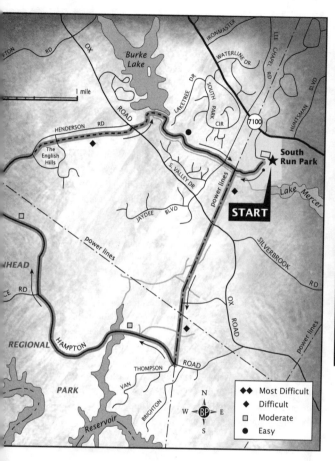

Ride Information

Trail Maintenance Hotline:
South Run Recreation Center:
(703) 644-7070
Fairfax County Park Authority:
(703) 246-5741

Schedule:
South Run Recreation Center is
open from 6 a.m. – 9 p.m., seven
days a week

Maps:
USGS maps: Fairfax, VA;
Occoquan, VA
ADC maps: Northern Virginia road
map
DeLorme: Virginia Atlas &
Gazetteer; Page 76 B-3

Fountainhead Regional Park in which nature trails take hikers
more than 18 miles to Bull Run, near the Manassas National
Battlefield. You then pick up an equestrian trail paralleling
Henderson Road as you continue to roll past million-dollar estates.
The route takes a fun little trail through the woods at Route 123,
then up to Burke Lake Dam for an incredible view of Northern
Virginia's largest lake. If you're up to it, follow the dirt bike path
around the lake. Otherwise, take the asphalt path back to South
Run Park, and ask yourself how you might one day own a house
like those along Hampton and Henderson Road.

Accotink Trail

Ride Specs

Start: Wakefield Park Recreation Center
Length: 6.1 miles
Rating: Easy
Terrain: Singletrack/dirt trails
Other Uses: Hiking

Getting There

From the **Capital Beltway (495)** – Exit **West on Braddock Road (Exit 5).** In less than 0.2 miles, turn **right** on **Wakefield Park's** Entrance Road. Go 0.6 miles to parking and **Recreation Center** on the left. Phones, water, toilets, and food available.

Sometimes it's interesting to see where you find singletrack. Typically, great mountain bike trails lie west or far north of the Washington suburbs. Out there—typically a "long drive" from where most of us live—singletrack and forest roads trace the landscape in all directions. The dirt's the limit. "If only we lived closer to the trails," goes the suburban cyclist's woeful anthem.

But a closer look reveals we do live near the trails—thanks to the Fairfax County Park Authority. Wakefield and Lake Accotink Parks, less than half a mile from the Capital Beltway in Fairfax County, are filled with a network of fun, technical singletrack. Most of these singletrack trails are offshoots from the park's main loop, which is a scenic, wooded dirt trail around Accotink's beautiful 70-acre lake.

The Accotink Trail itself was once part of Orange and Alexandria Railroad's original roadbed built in the early 1850s. The rails and ties, of course, have since been removed, and a new rail was laid farther south along a straighter route.

Lake Accotink's history began in the 1930s when the U.S. Army Corps of Engineers dammed Accotink Creek to create a reservoir for Fort Belvoir, nearly five miles downstream. The lake and surrounding land was given to Fairfax County in 1965 by the federal government for park and recreational use. The park's great trails, open to bicycling, have been "maturing" ever since.

This ride begins from Wakefield Park and travels south along the Accotink Trail around the lake, then back to Wakefield. There are even some great trails that go north from Wakefield and cross challenging routes beneath the power lines.

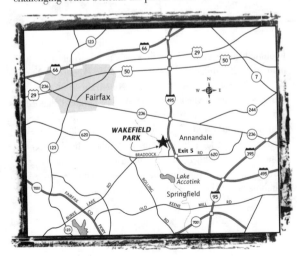

MilesDirections

0.0 START at Wakefield Park Recreation Center near the big green recycling bins. The trail begins up near the park entrance road and heads south through Wakefield toward Braddock Road.
0.2 Cross the athletic fields parking lot. Accotink Trail continues on the other side of the parking lot.
0.6 Cross under Braddock Road.
0.7 Just across Braddock Road, bear left, continuing on the main trail.
1.0 Stay left at the fork in the trail and follow the wooden Accotink Trail post.
2.1 Trail comes to a "T." Turn right, following Accotink Trail. The creek should be on your right. This part of the trail winds up and down through the woods. A lot of fun.
2.9 Arrive at Lake Accotink's marina.

Concessions, food, drinks, putt-putt golf, canoe and boat rental, etc.

Stay right, crossing the parking lot toward the dam.

3.0 Cross Lake Accotink Dam. Following the bike path, which parallels the train trestle, head toward the woods opposite the dam.
3.3 Re-enter the woods, up a steep climb, on Accotink Trail.

(continues on next page)

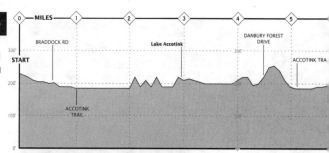

MilesDirections *(continued)*

4.5 Turn hard right off the dirt path on an asphalt trail, which takes you down on Danbury Forest Drive in the neighborhood of Danbury Forest. Kings Glen Elementary School on the right.

4.9 Re-enter Accotink Trail on the right just after Lonsdale Drive. This is a steep descent alongside the concrete steps into the woods.

5.0 Turn right off the asphalt path, following Accotink Trail across a wooden footbridge over Accotink creek.

5.1 Turn left on Accotink Trail.

5.5 Cross under Braddock Road.

6.1 Arrive back at the parking lot of Wakefield's Recreation Center

In Addition...

For those of you who just hopped off the beltway to reach this ride, here are some interesting tidbits about our capital city.

A thirteen-story city: For those who have been stuck on 395 north crossing the 14th Street Bridge during rush hour and never noticed—Washington, DC, has no skyline. The tallest buildings in the city are the Capitol and the Washington Monument. It is no accident, however, that the nation's capital doesn't have a single structure measuring higher than 130 feet. When Pierre L'Enfant designed this city at the end of the eighteenth century, he dreamt of a nation's capital filled with meaning and symbolism.

The Capitol, he envisioned, would represent the people of this land, standing taller than any other structure in the city. There is a law forbidding any structure in the area except the Washington Monument to rise above it. This ensures the building that represents the people of this nation can be seen from as far away as possible.

Higher learning:
It's no secret that Washington, DC, is the

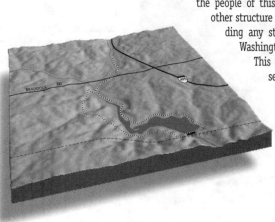

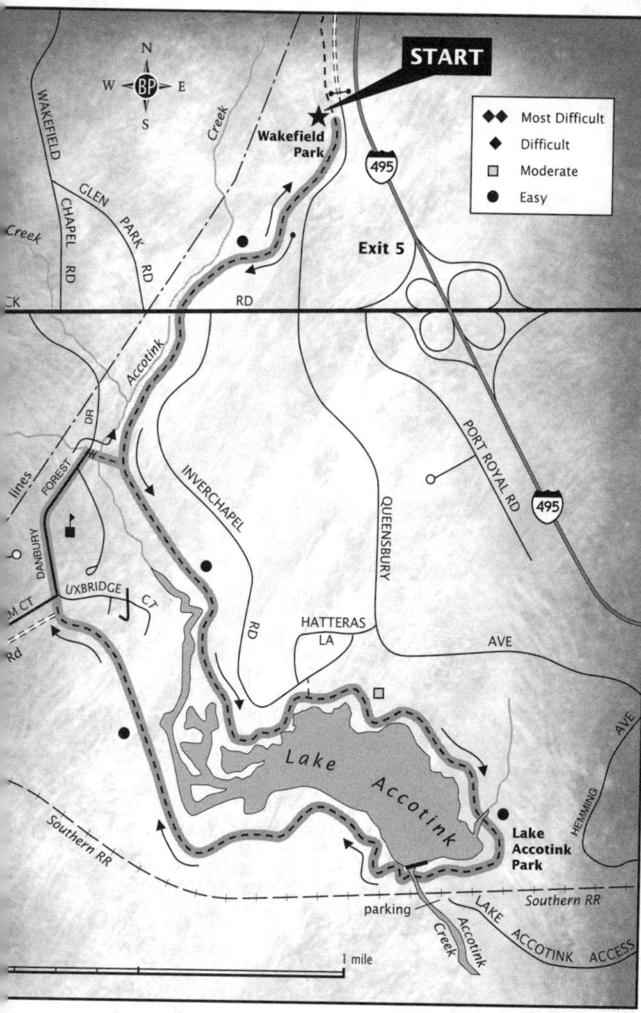

Ride Information

Trail Maintenance Hotline:
Fairfax County Park Authority:
(703) 246-5700
Lake Accotink Park:
(703) 569-3464

Schedule:
Open daylight to dark all year-round

Maps:
USGS maps: Annandale, VA
ADC map: Northern Virginia road map
DeLorme: Virginia Atlas & Gazetteer; Page 76 B-4
Fairfax County Park Authority trail map

epicenter of democracy, attracting people from all over the world to its bustling economy, policy-shaping influence, and high-tech industries. Those who come here to work and live also bring with them a strong value for higher learning. The Washington metropolitan area has two times the national average of college-educated adults, a large portion of whom also have graduate degrees. The area is considered to be, hands down, the most educated place to live in the United States, home to 18 universities and institutes of higher learning, including Georgetown, American, Howard, Johns Hopkins, and Gallaudet universities

Burke Lake Loop

Ride Specs

Start: South Run Park Recreation Center
Length: 7.3 miles
Rating: Easy
Terrain: Flat; asphalt,dirt trails
Other Uses: Hiking, nature observance, picnic, marina, boat launch, fishing

Getting There

From the **Capital Beltway (495)** – Take **I-95 south** toward **Richmond.** Go only about 0.5 miles and take **Springfield Exit 57, Route 644 west (Old Keene Mill Road)**. Follow Old Keene Mill Road west 3 miles, then turn **left** on **Huntsman Blvd.** Follow Huntsman Blvd 1.5 miles to the **Fairfax County Parkway.** Turn **right** on the Fairfax County Parkway, go about 0.3 miles and turn **left** into **South Run District Park**. Parking, water, phones, toilets, and showers.

*T*his spring the government chose Burke for the new airport. The whole town was shocked. 4,500 acres has been condemned. The town hasn't been the same since. Over 100 families are forced to find new homes by May 1, 1952.

Virginia Lee Fowler
October 11, 1951

This was the mood of the people of Burke, who were told in the early 1950s that the United States Government planned to build a huge space-age airport in the town of Burke, Virginia. Had it not been for some great leaders in the town's fight against this proposal, what is now Dulles Airport would have been built on the exact parcel of land you see in this map. Having lost the battle, the U.S. government reconsidered its original plan and decided instead on a large tract of undeveloped land in Chantilly. As we know, Dulles Airport is one of the nation's largest international ports, with regularly scheduled flights by the awesome 747 passenger jets and the supersonic Concord—how different things would have been.

Instead, the government publicly auctioned the parcels of land set aside for the original Burke Airport site on Saturday, June 13, 1959. Nearly 900 acres were given to the Fairfax County Park Authority, who, in the 1960s, dammed streams and flooded 218 acres to create Burke Lake.

This ride begins behind the field house at South Run Park and follows South Run north to Burke Lake. Unique and colorful gar-

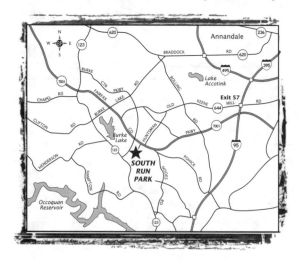

dens grow along the South Run trail, tilled by the residents of South Park Circle.

Surrounded by wooded parkland, it's easy to agree that Burke Lake, Fairfax County's largest lake, is also one of the region's

MilesDirections

0.0 START at South Run Park behind South Run Recreation Center (main building at park). Follow the paved path, starting behind the field house, down the hill into the woods.

0.2 Reach the bottom of the hill and follow the asphalt bike path along South Run. The stream should be on your left.

0.4 Cross underneath the power lines.

0.6 Cross underneath Lee Chapel Road.

1.5 Arrive at Burke Lake and turn left, crossing the dam.

1.7 Reach the other side of the dam. Continue along the gravel Bicycle & Walking Path, following the Park Trail signs.

2.0 Reach a small parking lot and boat ramp at the end of the cove. Follow the Park Trail signs.

2.2 Cross a small open field. Stay to the right side of the field. The trail picks up on the other side. (Trail markings are obscure here, so keep a sharp eye.)

2.4 Cross the park road leading to Burke Lake Park's Marina. Follow the Park Trail signs across the road, back into the woods.

Concession stand with food and drinks, boat rentals, bathrooms, etc. at the marina.

Stay left on the trail, going around the Frisbee golf course.

(continues on next page)

MilesDirections *(continued)*

3.3 The trail drops out on the paved park road. Turn right on this road, cross the bridge, then re-enter the trail back into the woods. (Burke Lake Road is on your left). Continue following the trail around the lake.

6.0 Reach the dam. The loop around Burke Lake is complete. Stay to the left and follow the asphalt bicycle path along South Run back to South Run Park.

7.1 Cross underneath the power lines.

7.3 Bear left up the asphalt path to South Run Park.

7.5 Reach South Run Park's Recreation Center.

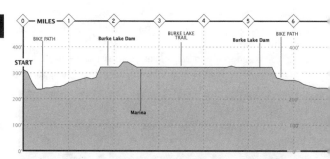

prettiest, most peaceful places for a bike ride. The gravel and dirt trail around the lake is flat—meandering along the shoreline. From this trail, you can view hundreds of birds as they come and go to their temporary home during the spring and fall migrations.

This ride does not have to start at South Run Park, of course, and can easily be altered to begin at Burke Lake. But be prepared for a $3.50 fee charged per car to nonresidents of Fairfax County.

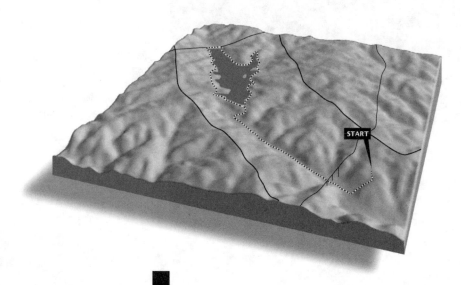

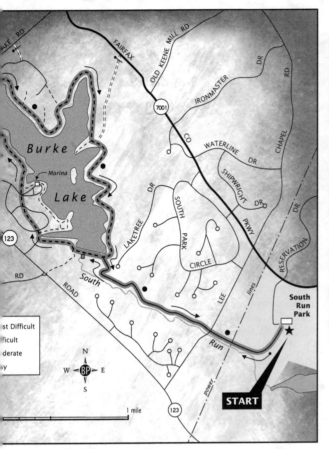

Ride Information

Trail Maintenance Hotline:
Fairfax County Park Authority:
(703) 246-5700
Burke Lake Park:
(703) 323-6600

Costs:
$3.50 per car for nonresidents of
Fairfax County at Burke Lake

Schedule:
Open daily from dawn to dusk,
mid-March to mid-November.
Trail is open year-round

Maps:
USGS: Fairfax, VA; Occoquan, VA
ADC map: Northern VA road map
DeLorme: Virginia Atlas &
   Gazetteer; Page 76 B-3
Burke Lake Park trail map

Fountainhead State Park

3

T hanks to the hard work of local advocacy groups, Virginians now have a host of new trails available for mountain biking. The Fountainhead Regional Park Mountain Bike Trail is one of them. Located in southern Fairfax County, in proximity to the Occoquan River, this trail offers a wide variety of terrain for riders of all skill levels.

The Doag Indians were the first to inhabit this area because of its abundance of natural resources, calling it "Occoquan," meaning *at the end of the water*, because of its proximity to the river. As with most Eastern American Indians, The Doags soon succumbed to English settlers, leaving the name Occoquan as one of the few legacies of their existence. During the Civil War this area served as a strategic line of defense between the north and the south. Such famous battlegrounds as Bull Run are just upstream.

Today, the area serves as part of the larger Bull Run Recreation Area and is managed by the Northern Virginia Regional Park Authority (NVRPA). This off-road bicycling trail is the first of its kind for mountain bikers. The NVRPA envisions it as an example for the region—a pilot program of sorts. If no user conflicts arise from this experiment, the NVRPA will consider opening more trails in the region for off-road cyclists. Let's set a good example here and help ensure the growth and acceptance of off-road bicycling trails in this region.

Your ride starts in the main parking lot as you head toward the marina. From the lot, pedal toward the trail entrance (staging area). This trail is has one-way traffic only, so don't plan to travel it in reverse. After a brief, fast, and technical downhill, you

Ride Specs

Start: Fountainhead Park
Length: 4.5 miles
Rating: Moderate to Difficult
Terrain:
Singletrack/Doubletrack
Other Uses: Hiking, marina, boat launch, swimming, fishing, horseback riding, snack bar, camping

Getting There

From the **Capital Beltway (495)** – Take **Exit 5 west** on **Braddock Road.** Head **south** on **Route 123.** Continue past Burke Lake Park to the **Fountainhead Park** sign on the **right side of the road.** Turn **right** at this sign on **Hampton Road.** Follow Hampton Road to the **park entrance on the left.** Park in the first parking lot on the right. The trailhead is to your **left.**

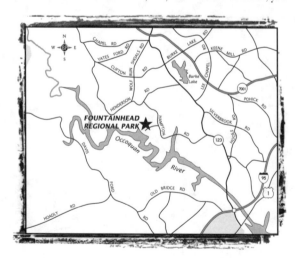

MilesDirections

0.0 START at the red trail trailhead, which is approximately 10 yards to the left of the "Nature Trail."

0.2 Turn left at this intersection and continue downhill toward the creek crossing. The trail, clearly marked as a **"BIKE TRAIL,"** briefly joins a hiking trail.

0.26 Take a left before a major creek crossing. Remember this is a one-directional trail. This is the only way to go. On your way back, you will have to negotiate Shockabilly Hill with its steep drop-offs. This is visible on the other side of the creek.

0.35 Cross the small creek and continue following the red blazes. Get ready to climb.

0.5 After a series of twists and one challenging ascent, turn left at the trail intersection, continuing down a gradual descent. Pay close attention to the exposed roots and stumps—unless you want to sample the soil! Turning right will take you to Shockabilly Hill.

0.84 There is a sharp sudden left switchback toward the bottom of the hill. Continue following the red blazes away from the reservoir. Do not go across the creek.

0.86 Turn right at this point and cross the small creek. Continue back toward the reservoir.

0.9 After a short steep hill you will be directly across from the previous switchback. Continue left, following the red blazes. The direction is clearly marked.

(continues on next page)

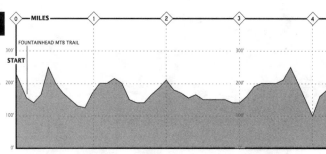

MilesDirections *(continued)*

1.16 Continue following the trail signs and red blazes.

1.37 Turn right at this trail intersection. The trail to the right is an equestrian-only trail.

1.53 Turn left, following the trail toward the "Optional Dead End Loop." Prepare for a fun descent. This is a two-way section, so be careful.

1.61 Bear right onto the single-track. After a twisty descent, the trail curves to the left, offering a great view of the reservoir.

2.1 You have completed the "Optional Dead End Loop." Turn right and continue up the two-way traffic section of trail.

2.2 Turn left at this intersection and continue down a fast descent. Keep alert, because you will have to abruptly turn left.

2.3 Follow the trail to the left.

2.4 Follow the switchback to the right. The trail continues to be blazed red.

(continues on next page)

will bear left at the first trail intersection. Be sure to always avoid the right fork in this trail—EQUESTRIANS/HIKERS ONLY. A small technical stream crossing leads you to the first turn and the beginning of the loop. The trail takes you around and back on a series of small loops offering up to five miles of technical, challenging singletrack. If, after your first or second loop, you're still up for it, head out to the marina and rent a boat or even play a game of miniature golf.

While you're here, don't miss the quaint, historic downtown of Occoquan, rich with history, antique shops, arts and crafts, and great restaurants. Visit the nation's first automated gristmill, and check out a host of historic homes and businesses, some of which have been in operation for over 200 years.

The Fountainhead Trail Project—A Ground-Breaking Event

The Fountainhead Regional Park Mountain Bike Trail was opened in the spring of 1997. Until then, bicycles were not permitted on any of the trails in the park. The trail is a single-direction trail, clearly marked with trail signs and red blazes. If at any point the red blazes are on the back of the trees rather than on the front, then you are going in the wrong direction and should turn around.

As mentioned earlier, the Fountainhead Regional Park Mountain Bike Trail represents an important opportunity and major breakthrough for cyclists in the Washington, DC metropolitan area. It was planned by the Northern Virginia Regional Park Authority (NVRPA) in close collaboration with the Mid-Atlantic Off-Road Enthusiasts (MORE), and initially funded, in large part, by Recreation Equipment,

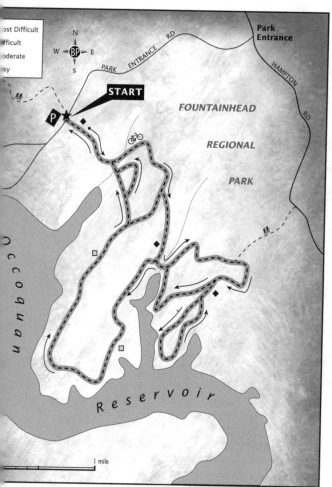

Ride Information

Trail Maintenance Hotline:
Northern Virginia Regional Park
  Authority: (703) 352-5900
Fountainhead Regional Park
(703) 250-9124
MORE (703) 502-0359

Costs:
$3.50 per car for nonresidents of
Fairfax County at Burke Lake

Schedule:
Open daily from dawn to dusk.
March to November

Maps:
USGS: Occoquan, VA
ADC map: Northern VA road map
DeLorme: Virginia Atlas &
  Gazetteer; Page 76 C-3

MilesDirections (continued)

2.66 Follow the trail to the left at another sign pointing to the parking lot. Go over the small wooden bridge and continue following the red blazes.

4.16 Reach Shockabilly Hill. Continue straight down this hill ONLY if you are an expert. These directions lead you to the right, following the "easier" alternate route.

4.3 Turn right over the wooden bridge. At this point, if you choose, turn right immediately after the bridge and do the loop again. If not, continue straight toward the red/yellow blazes.

4.35 Turn right over the small wooden bridge.

4.5 Arrive back at the trailhead.

Incorporated (REI). This flagship mountain bike trail project was designed specifically by mountain bikers for mountain bikers and will serve as a real litmus test for other park officials watching closely who may be interested in constructing and maintaining mountain bike-specific trailways at their parks.

A paved trailhead and two-way access trail is lined with split-rail fence to resist erosion and discourage "trail braiding." The trail was designed to take advantage of the area's elevation and terrain, and water bars are widely employed on its steeper grades, including new rubber belt-style devices popular in California. Overall trail usage is expected to be very high, quite possibly exceeding 500 users per month. Please take extreme measures when riding here to ensure this trail's success and durability. The trail is built. Now it's our turn to make sure it stays open.

Prince William Forest

Ride Specs

Start: Prince William Forest Park Visitors Center
Length: Various, depending on route chosen.(There are 8.2 miles of unpaved roads open to cyclists).
Rating: Moderate
Terrain: Hilly; Paved and unpaved park roads

Getting There

From the **Capital Beltway (495)** – Take **I-95 south** toward **Richmond** for 20 miles to **Exit 150, VA Route 619 west (Joplin Road)**. Turn **right** from Joplin Road in one-tenth of a mile to the **Park Entrance Road**. The **Visitors Center** is about one mile down this road. Telephone, bathroom, park information and trail maps here.

A t one time Prince William's thousands of acres of forestland was extensively farmed for tobacco. Then when the hills eroded and the earth could no longer support their crops, farmers turned to dairy farming, already well established throughout the county. But this too failed for those living in the Quantico Creek area. The Civil War was equally taxing for those already struggling here. The Confederates blockaded the Potomac, requiring large numbers of troops for support. Those living in the vicinity of the blockade were required to provide the troops with timber and food and found that what little they had before the war was no longer enough.

A mining operation near the confluence of the north and south branches of Conduce Creek provided a much-needed boost to the area's economy in 1889. But a strike over wages closed the high-grade pyrite ore mine in 1920, bringing down with it any hope for the area's recovery. It was soon thereafter that the United States Government bought the land, resettling nearly 150 families, and with the Civilian Conservation Corps began the effort to "return the depleted land to an ecological balance."

Prince William Forest Park now offers all kinds of outdoor activities for haggled Washingtonians to enjoy, one of which is bicycling. Riding on park trails, unfortunately, is prohibited. However, there are many unpaved, dirt roads throughout the park that can be used by cyclists. Many of these roads are separate out-and-back fire roads, in which case you may need to ride along the paved Scenic Drive Road to create loops. Scenic Drive Road is very well maintained and even has its own bike lane.

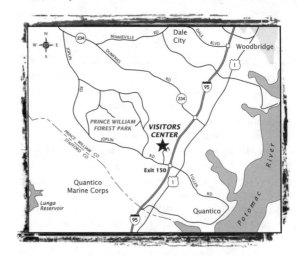

MilesDirections

Liming Lane Fire Road 0.8 miles long. This forest road is, for the most part, moderately easy. It begins from the parking lot on Scenic Drive Road and takes you out of the park's boundaries to Joplin Road.

Taylor Farm Road 1.5 miles long. From the northern part of Scenic Drive Road, Taylor Farm Road is mostly level until it drops sharply to the South Branch Quantico Creek. The first nine-tenths of this road are part of the 9.7-mile South Valley Trail, which travels the circumference of this region of Prince William Forest Park.

Burma Road 1.5 miles long. Burma Road starts out as an easy forest road, then crosses over a series of hills, making this section moderately difficult. This forest road crosses Quantico Creek and takes you to Pleasant Road. From here, you have the possibility to create a loop back to Scenic Drive Road. Following Pleasant Road past Cabin Camp you can gather "fool's gold" at the site of the old pyrite mine. Cross Quantico Creek again and take Pyrite Mine Road back to Scenic Drive Road.

(continues on next page)

Pyrite Mine Road 1.0 miles long.
This forest road takes you from
Scenic Drive Road to Quantico
Creek, the North Valley Trail, and
the old pyrite mine. The trail is
moderate in the beginning, then
becomes steep at the end.

**North Orenda Road 1.2 miles
long.** This is a moderate forest
road that takes you down to the
South Branch. Across the creek is
South Orenda Fire Road that leads
you back to the visitors center.

Lake One Road 0.6 miles long.
Lake One Road starts from the
parking lot along Scenic Drive
Road and takes you down a moderately steep hill to Quantico Creek.

**Old Black Top Road 1.6 miles
long.** Old Black Top Road starts
from the Turkey Run Parking area
and travels north, crossing Taylor
Farm Road, then connects with
Scenic Drive Road. The terrain is
moderate and offers a good challenge through the middle
of the park.

Road cyclists from all around often come to Prince William Forest
Park just to ride this paved loop through the forest and get quite a
workout from its hills.

To witness the absolute
progress the forest has made in
reclaiming what was once
depleted and eroding farmland
is a wonderful experience when
you visit this 18,000-acre forest.
And riding your mountain bike
along the forest roads through
the park gives you an up-close
look at this process in action.

It's hard, though, to really get
away from it all in this metropolitan area no matter how hard
you try. And this point is never
more evident than to drive a bit
farther south on I-95 to one of
Virginia's greatest tourist attrac-
tions—Potomac Mills shopping
center, a destination shopping
attraction that brings in over
13,000 bus tours each year.
Potomac Mills was reported in
the Washington Post on
September 8, 1991, as the top-
rated tourist attraction in the
state of Virginia ahead of both Colonial Williamsburg and Busch
Gardens—and claims it continues to hold that rating!

With more than 52 acres of parking and
1.7 million square feet of
fully enclosed shopping
space, it's easy to
understand how this
super-regional special-
ty mall brings in the
foot traffic. Their mix-
ture of outlet stores and
off-price retailers draw
cost-conscious shoppers
from around the globe to

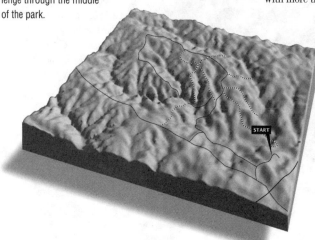

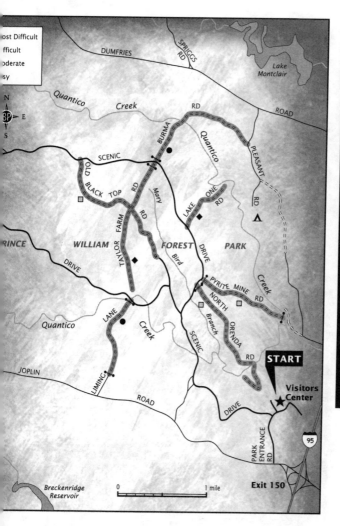

Ride Information

Trail Maintenance Hotline:
Prince William Forest Park
Visitors Center:
(703) 221-7181
National Park Service
(703) 759-2915

Costs:
$3.00 per vehicle within the park

Schedule:
Visitors Center open between 8:30
a.m. and 5:00 p.m.

Maps:
USGS maps: Joplin, VA;
Quantico, VA, MD
ADC maps: Prince William
County road map
DeLorme: Virginia Atlas &
    Gazetteer; Page 76 D-3
Prince William Forest Park trail
    map

its market. It's really somewhat bewildering to wander Potomac Mills' crowded walkways past its hundreds of shops and thousands of people. The thought of getting back on the bike and pedaling to Prince William Forest becomes all the more enticing. But hey, if you're down in the area anyway, why not head to the largest, most crowded single-floor shopping mall on the planet? Buy some Power Bars and Lycra shorts, then head back north and hit the trails.

Fort Circle Trails

3

Getting There

From the **Capital Beltway (495)** – Exit **North on MD Route 5 (Branch Avenue) toward Washington.** Go 2.8 miles, then turn **left on Suitland Parkway.** Go 1.8 miles and then turn **right** at the light on **Stanton Road.** Take the immediate **right** up **Gainesville Street,** then **left up 18th Street.** At the top of the hill, turn **right** on **Erie Street** and park at the **Smithsonian Museum of African-American History.** Phone, water, toilets.

From the **Baltimore-Washington Parkway (Kenilworth Avenue (295))** – Exit **West** on **Suitland Parkway.** Go 1.2 miles, turn **left** at the first light on **Stanton Road.** Continue with directions above.

A fter Confederates overwhelmingly defeated the Union army at the first battle of Manassas in July 1861, Union General George McClellan, aware of Washington's vulnerability, ordered heavy fortifications built around the virtually defenseless Union capital. Then, Fort Washington, nearly 12 miles down river, was all that guarded Washington. But by the spring of 1865, a ring of 68 forts, 93 batteries, and nearly 200 cannons and mortars surrounded the capital, making it the most heavily fortified city in the nation.

The only challenge to Washington's defenses came in July 1864, with a daring attack by Confederate General Jubal A. Early. Choosing a route through the northern perimeter of the city's defense, Early fought his way from Frederick, Maryland, to Silver Spring. But Union forces rushed reinforcements to the northern garrisons above Washington and successfully routed Early's troops. The Confederates were forced to retreat across the Potomac at Whites Ferry and Edwards Ferry, ending the first and only action against the city.

Most of the forts and batteries were dismantled after the Civil War, and the land returned to its prewar

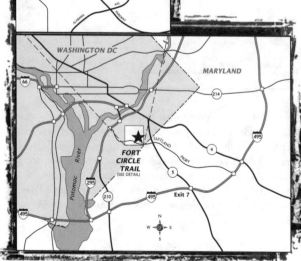

MilesDirections

0.0 START in the parking lot of Anacostia's Smithsonian Museum for Africa-American History. Cross Erie Street to the open grassy area opposite the parking lot. Staying right of the dirt road next to Fort Stanton Park's swimming pool, follow the thin dirt path diagonally across the field up into the woods. (Entrance into the woods is at the far right corner of the field). Follow this trail into the woods no more than 20 feet before turning sharp left down a steep singletrack trail.

0.2 End of descent. Cross a wooden foot bridge over the creek.

0.5 Cross Good Hope Road. Follow Park Services Hiker-Biker trail sign across the street. This is a paved trail for the first 100 feet, then changes back to dirt and gravel.

0.9 Cross Naylor Avenue. Hiker-Biker trail is directly across the street, slightly to the right.

1.2 Cross 28th Street SouthEast. Hiker-Biker trail entrance is to the left.

1.6 Exit trail on Park Drive SouthEast and turn left. Follow this for one block to Branch Avenue. Cross Branch Avenue. Hiker-Biker trail entrance is to the left.

2.1 Cross Pennsylvania Avenue. Entrance to Fort Davis Park. Bear left at the entrance, continuing on Hiker-Biker trail down into the woods.

2.7 Trail turns into asphalt. Cross Fort Davis Road.

(continues on next page)

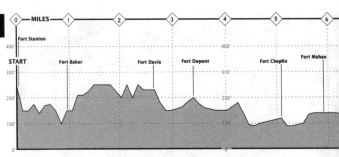

MilesDirections *(continued)*

2.9 Cross Massachusetts Avenue. Continue straight on Hiker-Biker trail dirt and gravel. Enter Fort Dupont Park.

3.5 Trail forks. Turn left at the first fork, taking the Lower trail. (Right will take you up to Fort Dupont – 0.5 miles).

3.7 Trail comes to a "T." Turn left, horseshoeing slightly downhill. Ridge Road should remain above you on your right.

4.4 Trail exits at the intersection of Fort Davis Road and Ridge Road. Hiker-Biker trail sign is catty corner across this intersection. Cross the Fort Davis Road-Ridge Road intersection. The trail entrance at this point is somewhat overgrown. Keep your eyes peeled.

4.9 Cross C Street. The Hiker-Biker trail entrance is to the right.

5.1 Trail splits. Bear left at this split.

5.2 Trail comes to a "T." Turn right.

(continues on next page)

owners. Nonetheless, remains of several of these fortifications were preserved by the National Park Service and now make up what is known as the Fort Circle Parks. Among those under the care of the National Park Service are several forts built on hilltops overlooking the Anacostia River. Fort Mahan, Fort Chaplin, Fort Dupont, Fort Davis, and Fort Stanton were some of the strongholds guarding over Capitol Hill.

Today, the corridor between these forts along the Anacostia River makes a wonderful greenway, complete with a well maintained and clearly marked hiker-biker trail that connects Fort Stanton with Fort Mahan. Long sections of narrow singletrack and twisting trails take you up and down the steep hills on which each fort was built. Cyclists, however, must allow plenty of daylight for this ride and should study directions and maps carefully before starting. While this trail winds through a forested oasis, it's also in some of Washington's rougher neighborhoods, notorious for their high crime rates. Be safe, wear your armor, and have fun, because this is absolutely one of Washington's greatest mountain bike rides!

In Addition...

Washington, DC, is one of only a few planned cities in the world. Designed by Pierre L'Enfant, the cornerstone for the city was laid in 1793. Its original design in the shape of a diamond was created to be both geometrically and geographically precise. In 1847, however, the southwest quadrant was returned to Virginia. The city centers on the Washington Monument, where the north-south and east-west axes of the diamond converge. The Potomac River separates the city from Virginia on the southwest side,

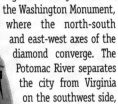
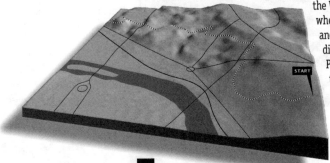

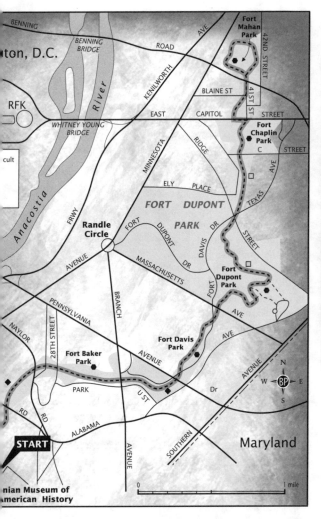

MilesDirections (continued)

5.3 Cross East Capitol Street. Be careful of traffic. Take the crosswalk to the right. Then follow the Hiker-Biker trail sign up the hill, back into the woods.

5.6 Exit trail on 41st Street.

5.7 Cross Benning Street. Go straight up the unmarked embankment to the asphalt path and turn left. Follow this trail around as it does a full circle around Fort Mahan Park.

6.6 Arrive back at Benning Street and 41st Street. Follow the Hiker-Biker trail signs back along the Fort Circle Trail to where you started at the Smithsonian's African-American History Museum.

while Maryland borders the northwest, northeast, and southeast sides of the city. The district's other major river, the Anacostia, flows through the southeastern part of the city into the Potomac and eventually the Chesapeake Bay. The entire area of Washington, DC, measures nearly 69 square miles while the constantly growing metropolitan area measures in at more than 400 square miles. Today estimates bring the Washington/Baltimore area population at close to 6.9 million people, making it the fourth largest metropolitan area in the United States.

C&O Canal

Ride Specs

Start: Georgetown Visitors Center
Length: 184 miles one way
Rating: Easy
Terrain: Flat canal towpath (mostly dirt or crushed stone)
Other Uses: Hiking, horseback riding, camping, rollerblading

Getting There

From the **White House** – Take **Pennsylvania Avenue NW** toward **Georgetown.** Go 11 blocks to **M Street**, **turn left** into Georgetown, and go two blocks to Thomas Jefferson Street. **Turn left on Thomas Jefferson Street. C&O Canal Visitor Center** here.

From the **Metro** – Take the Metro to **Foggy Bottom Metro station (Orange and Blue lines)**. Go **north** on **23rd Street** two blocks to **Washington Circle.** Go counterclockwise on Washington Circle to Pennsylvania Avenue NW. Take **Pennsylvania Avenue NW** five blocks to **Georgetown.** From here, follow the directions above.

O n a hot Fourth of July in Washington, DC, 1828, ground was broken and the challenge under way to see who would reach the western "frontier" (Wheeling, West Virginia) first. The competitors—the Chesapeake & Ohio Canal Company versus the Baltimore & Ohio Railroad. Both started digging the same day. Through high costs, floods, land-access problems, 185 miles of rugged earth along the Potomac River, and 22 years of backbreaking labor, the C&O canal finally reached Cumberland, Maryland—eight years after the B&O. Nevertheless, 11 stone aqueducts, 74 lift locks, and 185 miles of canal were complete.

(The remainder of the route to Wheeling, West Virginia, would be by road.) Unfortunately, not only did the railroad reach the west first, but also was faster and more reliable, as floods, freezes, and drought often handicapped the canal. Losing money to the railroad and regularly repairing costly flood damage, the C&O canal was forced to close its gates in 1924, less than 100 years after its completion.

Today, however, it is one of the most successful and reliable resources in the nation. Its success comes not in profits, though,

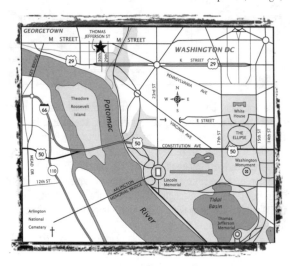

but in the pleasure it provides to the thousands who hike, bike, or horseback along the crushed-stone-and natural-surfaced towpath each year. It is a reliable treasure chest of sights and wonders, delightful scenery, peace and solitude, and miles of serenity each day of the year. One of the best ways to enjoy the C&O Canal is to ride it in sections, beginning from different starting points. But there are plenty of camp sights along the towpath to accommo-

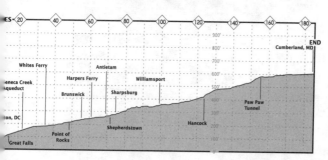

MilesDirections

0.0 START at the Georgetown Visitor Center at the corner of Thomas Jefferson Street and M Street in Georgetown.

3.1 Fletcher's Boat House on the left through the tunnel. Bike rentals and repairs.

14.3 Great Falls Tavern Visitor Center.

22.8 Seneca Creek Aqueduct.

30.8 Edwards Ferry. Not in operation.

35.5 Whites Ferry. Last operating ferry on the Potomac.

42.2 Monocacy Aqueduct. The largest aqueduct along the canal.

44.6 Nolands Ferry.

48.2 Point of Rocks. Food available along Clay Street (Route 28).

55.0 Town of Brunswick. Phone, food, and groceries.

60.8 Harpers Ferry. C&O Canal Park Headquarters. Phone, food, and grocery store. Cross Appalachian Trail.

69.3 Antietam Creek Aqueduct. Ranger Station and camp.

72.7 Shepherdstown. Phone, food, and groceries.

99.8 Williamsport. Phone, food, and groceries.

124.0 Hancock. Visitor Center. Phone, food, and groceries.

156.0 Paw Paw Tunnel.

184.5 Reach Cumberland. C&O Canal towpath ends here. Phone, food, groceries.

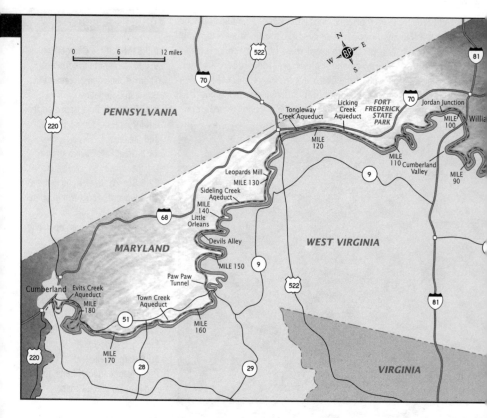

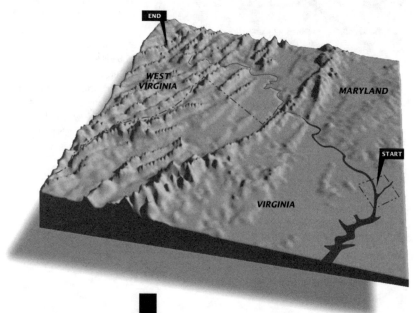

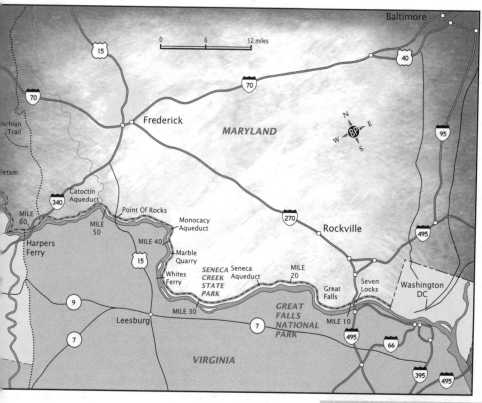

date a one-shot effort from Washington, DC, to Cumberland.

The surface of the towpath is mostly dirt or crushed stone and remains in excellent condition. Due to floods, freezes, and tree roots, however, you should be prepared for some bumpy trails. Also, be aware that after heavy rainfall and times of high water, some sections might be impassable. Just keep this in mind.

With regards to the maps, don't be fooled by this ride's profile. It looks like an uphill battle all the way to Cumberland. Over 185 miles, however, a 600-foot elevation gain is virtually unnoticeable, and the trail will seem absolutely flat.

Ride Information

Trail Maintenance Hotline:
C&O Canal Headquarters:
(301) 739-4200

Schedule:
Open from dawn til dusk every day of the year.

Maps:
DeLorme maps: Maryland road
map; Virginia road map
ADC maps: Washington, DC, road
map
National Park Service C&O Canal
trail map

Honorable Mentions

I t would be tough to map every one of the Washington/Baltimore area's off-road bicycle rides into a single guidebook. There are too many. Therefore, it is necessary to chart only the best bike rides the area has to offer, delegating other popular places for mountain biking to Honorable Mention status. And still, somehow, only a mere fraction of the area's rides are included. Compiled below is an index of great rides that did not make the A-list this time around, but deserve recognition. Check them out and let us know what you think. You may decide one or more of these rides deserves higher status in future editions or, perhaps, you may have a ride of you own that merits some attention.

A. Swallow Falls State Park.

Located in the far western panhandle of Maryland, nine miles northwest of Oakland in Garrett State Forest. Although occupying only 257 acres of Garret State Forest's 7,400 acres of land, visitors are treated to a 63-foot waterfall, spectacular scenery, nature trails, and the rapids of the Youghiogheny River. Cyclists will enjoy Swallow Falls' 11-mile round-trip trail system that connects the park's two sections. Formed from old logging roads and rail lines, mountain bikers and cross-country skiers enjoy the diverse terrain it has to offer—from hard-packed doubletrack to rocky singletrack. Swallow Falls State Park has fishing, boating, unrestricted camping, winter sports, and an historic area.

B. Wisp Ski Area.

Operating as a four-season resort for nearly 40 years, Wisp hasn't always been as hospitable to vacationers and recreationalists as it is today. Fifty years ago, Wisp was a towering and treeless mound of earth known only as Marsh Mountain. The only activity it saw was a herd of cattle grazing its slopes. Today, Helmuth Heise, his wife Evelyn, and several Garrett County businessmen can sit back and reflect on their successful efforts in transforming this area into a four-season vacation land. It continues to be one of the only continuous family owned and operated ski resorts in the country. For mountain bikers, hop on one of the chairlifts, go to the top, and ride down logging roads, ski trails, and rugged singletrack. There is a lift fee and a nominal admission fee. Stop by nearby High Mountain Sports to get a two-for-one coupon.

C. Whitetail Ski Resort.

Whitetail is in Pennsylvania, and therefore must have sneaked its way
this book as a Washington/Baltimore area mountain bike hot spot. It's
secret, however, that when the weather turns warm and the snow melts
y, Whitetail is transformed into one of the region's greatest mountain
resorts. Fully equipped with a fleet of top-end mountain bike rentals,
lifts to the top of Two Top Mountain, and singletrack trails all the way
n and around, Whitetail has cultivated itself into a local hub for met-
olitans looking for lots of legal and well-maintained singletrack. For
se interested in a long weekend of mountain biking coupled with pam-
ed lounging in the lodge, this is the most dedicated mountain bike
rt in town. Whitetail Resort is located in Mercersburg, PA, north of
erstown, MD, off I-70. For more information, call (717) 328-9400.

D. Frederick Watershed.

Just north of Frederick, Maryland, adjacent to Gambrill State Park,
erick Watershed is a fantastic mountain bike playground. There are
es of unpaved forest roads winding all over Catoctin Mountain, all of
ch are perfectly suitable for off-road bikes. The terrain is very steep and
ged, but if you're heading toward Gambrill or the Catoctin Blue Trail
way, take a small detour and check out the Frederick Watershed.

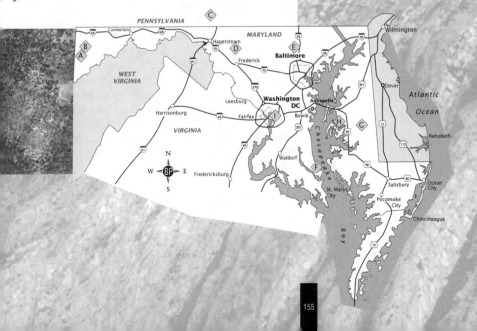

Honorable Mentions(Continued)

E. Gunpowder Falls (Sweet Air Area)

Located in Northern Maryland, the Sweet Air area of Gunpowder F
State Park has over nine miles of hiking, equestrian, and cycling trails. Fr
Baltimore, take I-95 north to Exit 74 (152 west). Follow 152 west for
miles, then turn left onto 165 (Baldwin Mill Road). Take your first right o
Green Road. Turn right on Moores Road, cross the single-lane bridge bef
turning left onto Dalton Road. Continue to the park entrance. The trailhe
is directly across form the large trail map. For more information call (4
592-2897.

F. Calvert Cliffs.

Located on the western side of the Chesapeake Bay, the cliffs at Calv
Cliffs State Park dominate the shoreline. Rising more than 100 feet from
shores of the Chesapeake, these 15 million-year-old cliffs contain over 6
species of fossils from the Miocene period. Calvert Cliffs State Park is loc
ed in Calvert County on Routes 2 and 4, 14 miles south of Prince Frederi
There are over 13 miles of foot and mountain bike trails here. Bicycles
allowed on the service road. For more information and directions to op
riding areas call Blue Wind in California, Maryland, at (301) 737-2713.

G. Tuckahoe State Park.

Located just east of Maryland's Bay Bridge in Talbott County, Tuckah
State Park has a surprisingly great trail system. The park has two main s
tions of trails. The first and longest is located below the dam and trav
parallel to Tuckahoe Creek. This trail switches between hiking trails, equ
trian trails and a wide hard-surface path. The second trail is far shorter a
runs along the creek above the lake. This section is far more challeng
than the lower trail, offering more obstacles and a few sharp drop-offs w
steep sections along gullies. For more information call or write Tuckah
State Park at 13070 Crouse Mill Road, Queen Anne, MD 21657—(410) 8
1668.

H. Wye Island Natural Resource Management Area.

Wye Island is located in Queen Anne's County near Queenstown, ryland. The Island is located between the Wye and Wye East Rivers in e tidal recesses of the Chesapeake Bay. 2,450 of the 2,800 acres are man- ed and maintained by the Department of Natural Resources and the ryland State and Park Forest Service. There are over six miles of trails, me of which are open to bicycles. For more information, call or write Wye and Natural Resources Management Area at 632 Wye Island Road, eenstown, MD 21658—(410) 827-7577.

I. Fort DuPont Park.

Located just east of the heart of Washington, DC, Fort DuPont Park is e site of a former Civil War fortress that overlooks the Anacostia River d RFK Stadium. Fort DuPont has nearly eight miles of twisting, hilly, oded trails. Fort DuPont Park is also the only park in the District of umbia that allows bikes on its trails. To get to the park take 395 north DC all the way to Pennsylvania Avenue SE. Cross the Sousa Bridge into acostia and turn left onto Minnesota Avenue. Continue on Minnesota enue to Randall Circle. The park entrance is on your right. Park in the ivity Center parking lot—first lot to the left. For more information call 2) 426-7723. One thing to do before heading out to Fort DuPont is to ke sure you've got plenty of daylight. While the park and surrounding t Circle Hiker/Biker trail is considered safe, it is always best to allow lots light for your travels.

Ski Resorts
[...for mountain biking?]

Ski resorts offer a great alternative local trail riding. During the spri summer, and fall, many resorts will op their trails for mountain biking and, j like during ski season, sell lift tickets take you and your bike to the top of mountain. Lodging is also available for the we end mountain bike junkies, and rates are oft discounted from the normal ski-season pric Some resorts will even rent bikes and lead gui mountain bike tours. Call ahead to find out j what each resort offers in the way of mount bike riding, and pick the one that best suits y fancy.

The following is a list of all the ski resc within 200 miles of the Washington/Baltim area that say **yes!** to mountain biking when weather turns too warm for skiing.

Massanutten
Harrisonburg, VA
(703) 289-9441

Wintergreen
Waynesboro, VA
(804) 325-2200

The Homestead
Hot Springs, VA
(703) 839-5500

Bryce
Basye, VA
(703) 856-2121

Wisp
McHenry, MD
(301) 387-4911

Timberline
Davis, WV
1-800-843-1751

Canaan Valley
Davis, WV
(304) 866-4121

Snowshoe
Marlinton, WV
(304) 572-1000

Whitetail
Mercersburg, PA
(717) 328-9400

Ski Liberty
Carroll Valley, PA
(717) 642-8282

Ski Roundtop
Lewisberry, PA
(717) 432-9631

Blue Knob
Claysburg, PA
(814) 239- 5111

Hidden Valley
Somerset, PA
(814) 443-6454

Seven Springs
Somerset, PA
1-800-452-2223

Fat Tire Vacations
[Bicycle Touring Companies]

There are literally dozens of off-ro
bicycling tour companies offering
incredible variety of guided tours f
mountain bikers. On these pay-as-yo
pedal, fat-tire vacations, you will have
chance to go places around the glo
that only an expert can take you, and your exp
riences will be so much different than if se
through the window of a tour bus.

From Hut to Hut in the Colorado Rockies
Inn to Inn through Vermont's Green Mountair
there is a tour company for you. Whether y
want hardcore singletrack during the day a
camping at night, or you want scenic trails f
lowed by a bottle of wine at night and a mint
each pillow, someone out there offers what you
looking for. The tours are well organized a
fully supported with   expert guides, bi
mechanics, and "sag wagons" which carry ge
food, and tired bodies. Prices range from $10
$500 for a weekend to more than $2000 for tw
week-long trips to far-off lands such as N
Zealand or Ireland. Each of these companies w
gladly send you their free literature to wh
your appetite with breathtaking photograp
and titillating stories of each of their tours.

lk River Touring Center
latyfork, WV
304) 572-3771

ermont Bicycling Touring
ristol, VT
-800-245-3868

ackroads
erkley, CA
-800-BIKE TRIP

imberline Bicycle Tours
enver, CO
303) 759-3804

Roads Less Traveled
Longmont, CO
(303) 678-8750

Blackwater Bikes
Davis, WV
(304) 259-5286

Bicycle Adventures
Olympia, WA
1-800-443-6060

Trails Unlimited, Inc.
Nashville, IN
(812) 988-6232

Selected Touring Companies

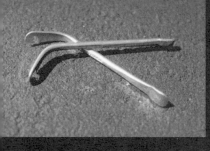

Appendix:Repair and Maintenance

FIXING A FLAT

TOOLS YOU WILL NEED

- Two tire irons
- Pump (either a floor pump or a frame pump)
- No screwdrivers!!! (This can puncture the tube)

REMOVING THE WHEEL

The front wheel is easy. Simply open the quick release mechanism or undo the bolts with the proper sized wrench, then remove the wheel from the bike.

The rear wheel is a little more tricky. Before you loosen the wheel from the frame, shift the chain into the smallest gear on the freewheel (the cluster of gears in the back). Once you've done this, removing and installing the wheel, like the front, is much easier.

REMOVING THE TIRE

Step one: Insert a tire iron under the bead of the tire and pry the tire over the lip of the rim. Be careful not to pinch the tube when you do this.

Step two: Hold the first tire iron in place. With the second tire iron, repeat step one, three or four inches down the rim. Alternate tire irons, pulling the bead of the tire over the rim, section by section, until one side of the tire bead is completely off the rim.

Step three: Remove the rest of the tire and tube from the rim. This can be done by hand. It's easiest to remove the valve stem last. Once the tire is off the rim, pull the tube out of the tire.

CLEAN AND SAFETY CHECK

Step four: Using a rag, wipe the inside of the tire to clean out any dirt, sand, glass, thorns, etc. These may cause the tube to puncture. The inside of a tire should feel smooth. Any pricks or bumps could mean that you have found the culprit responsible for your flat tire.

Step five Wipe the rim clean, then check the rim strip, making sure it covers the spoke nipples properly on the inside of the rim. If a spoke is poking through the rim strip, it could cause a puncture.

Step six: At this point, you can do one of two things: replace the punctured tube with a new one, or patch the hole. It's easiest to just replace the tube with a new tube when you're out

on the trails. Roll up the old tube and take it home to repair later that night in front of the TV. Directions on patching a tube are usually included with the patch kit itself.

INSTALLING THE TIRE AND TUBE *(This can be done entirely by hand)*

Step seven: Inflate the new or repaired tube with enough air to give it shape, then tuck it back into the tire.

Step eight: To put the tire and tube back on the rim, begin by putting the valve in the valve hole. The valve must be straight. Then use your hands to push the beaded edge of the tire onto the rim all the way around so that one side of your tire is on the rim.

Step nine: Let most of the air out of the tube to allow room for the rest of the tire.

Step ten: Beginning opposite the valve, use your thumbs to push

the other side of the tire onto the rim. Be careful not to pinch the tube in between the tire and the rim. The last few inches may be difficult, and you may need the tire iron to pry the tire onto the rim. If so, just be careful not to puncture the tube.

BEFORE INFLATING COMPLETELY

Step eleven: Check to make sure the tire is seated properly and that the tube is not caught between the tire and the rim. Do this by adding about 5 to 10 pounds of air, and watch closely that the tube does not bulge out of the tire.

Step twelve: Once you're sure the tire and tube are properly seated, put the wheel back on the bike, then fill the tire with air. It's easier squeezing the wheel through the brake shoes if the tire is still flat.

Step thirteen: Now fill the tire with the proper amount of air, and check constantly to make sure the tube doesn't bulge from the rim. If the tube does appear to bulge out, release all the air as quickly as possible, or you could be in for a big bang.

• *When installing the rear wheel,* place the chain back onto the smallest cog (furthest gear on the right), and pull the derailleur out of the way. Your wheel should slide right on.

LUBRICATION AVOIDS DETERIORATION

Lubrication is crucial to maintaining your bike. Dry spots will be eliminated. Creaks, squeaks, grinding, and binding will be gone. The chain will run quietly, and the gears will shift smoothly. The brakes will grip quicker, and your bike may last longer with fewer repairs. Need I say more? Well, yes. Without knowing where to put the lubrication, what good is it?

THINGS YOU WILL NEED

• One can of bicycle lubricant, found at any bike store.
• A clean rag (to wipe excess lubricant away).

WHAT GETS LUBRICATED

• Front derailleur
• Rear derailleur

- Shift levers
- Front brake
- Rear brake
- Both brake levers
- Chain

WHERE TO LUBRICATE

To make it easy, simply spray a little lubricant on all the pivot points of your bike. If you're using a squeeze bottle, use just a drop or two. Put a few drops on each point wherever metal moves against metal, for instance, at the center of the brake calipers. Then let the lube sink in.

Once you have applied the lubricant to the derailleurs, shift the gears a few times, working the derailleurs back and forth. This allows the lubricant to work itself into the tiny cracks and spaces it must occupy to do its job. Work the brakes a few times as well.

LUBING THE CHAIN

Lubricating the chain should be done after the chain has been wiped clean of most road grime. Do this by spinning the pedals counterclockwise while gripping the chain with a clean rag. As you add the lubricant, be sure to get some in between each link. With an aerosol spray, just spray the chain while pedalling backwards (counterclockwise) until the chain is fully lubricated. Let the lubricant soak in for a few seconds before wiping the excess away. Chains will collect dirt much faster if they're loaded with too much lubrication.

RepairAndMa

Area Clubs, Mountain Bike Clubs and Other Trail Groups

IMBA
(International Mountain Biking
Association)
2475 Broadway
Suite 100
Boulder CO 80304
303.545.9011
FAX: 303.545.9026
imba@aol.com
http://www.imba.com
(advocay)

MORE
(Mid Atlantic Off Road Enthusiasts)
P.O. Box 2662
Fairfax, VA 22031
703.502.0359
more@cycling.org
trailshead@aol.com
http://apollo.gmu.edu/~chain/more
(advocacy and riding club)

MAMBO
(Maryland Association of Mountain
Bike Operators)
319 Dixie Dr
Towson, MD 21204
410.337.BIKE
76371.2354@compuserve.com
http://ourworld.compuserve.com/hom
epages/vrmgt/mambo.htm
(advocacy and riding)

Capybara Mountain Bike Club
P.O. Box 3932
Crofton, MD 21114
410.674.3467
http://www.nmaa.org/member/capy-
bara
(advocacy and riding)

St. Mary's Mountain Biking Club
St. Mary's College
St. Mary's City, MD 20686
301.862.0209
301.862.0308

NORBA
(National Off Road Bicycle
Association)
One Olympic Plaza
Colorado Springs, CO 80909
719.578.4717
FAX: 719.578.4956
norba@usacycling.org
http://www.adventuresports.com/asa
p/norba/norba.htm
(racing)

League of American Bicyclists
190 West Ostend St.
Suite 120
Baltimore, MD 21230-3731
1.800.288.BIKE
FAX: 410.539.3496
http://bikeleague.org

Rails-to-Trails Conservancy
1100 17th St NW
10th Floor
Washington, DC 20036
202.331.9696
http://litwww.cwru.edu/lit/homes/rxr
3/WVRTC/JoinRTC.html

OTHER AREA BICYCLE CLUBS

REGIONAL

Potomac Pedalers Touring Club
6729 Curren St.
McLean VA 22101
703.442.8780
202.363.TOUR
http://blueridge.infomkt.ibm.com/bik
es/PPTC.html
(nation's largest local touring club)

WABA
(Washington Area Bicycling
Association)
818 Connecticut Ave
Suite 300
Washington DC 20006
202.872.9830

Washington Women Outdoors
PO Box 301
Garret Park, MD 20896-0301
301.864.3070
(offers day and overnight trips for
women)

MARYLAND

College Park Racing Team
4360 Knox Rd.
College Park, MD 20740
301.779.4848
(racing club)

College Park Bicycle Club
4360 Knox Rd.
College Park, MD 20740
301.779.4848

Oxon Hill Bicycle Club
PO Box 81
Oxon Hill Md 20750-0081
301.567.6760
(backcountry roads rides)

VIRGINIA

Reston Bicycle Club
PO Box 3389
Reston, VA 22090-1389
703.904.0900

Inde

T

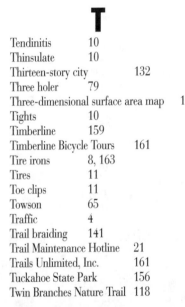

Meet the Authors

When not conquering fiery new trails on his mountain bike or racing from town to town on his road bike, Scott Adams is hard at work on his next guidebook, mastering the art of takeout, or exploring the backcountry with Porter, his loyal Chessie and slobbering companion. Scott is a native of Virginia who lives his life to be outdoors, but finds much of his time spent behind the monitor of a computer preparing the next set of maps or arranging for the next book in the series. Few things reward him more than a long hike to the top of a mountain or an early-morning bike ride with no particular place to go.

Martín Fernández is a native of Lima, Perú, and now lives in Montgomery County, Maryland. When he's not riding his FAT in the backcountry trails of Maryland, Martín is hard at work designing publications and web sites or trying to come up with an award winning homebrew recipe. He is a graphic designer who enjoys the freedom of cycling more than anything and ponders the question of what his next book will be. A novel perhaps?

BarMap mapcase is a simple,
~~ght~~ solution to this age-old
~~many~~ guidebook owners often
~~ce.~~ Its soft, clear mapcase vel-
~~ly~~ to the handlebar. Those days
~~g~~ maps out of your fanny pack,
~~g,~~ refolding, and stuffing them
~~are~~ forever in the past. Get the
~~t~~ the first time and leave the
~~the~~ car! **$7.95**

The Perfect Mountain Biking Companion

The Forest Hump™
by CycoActive Products

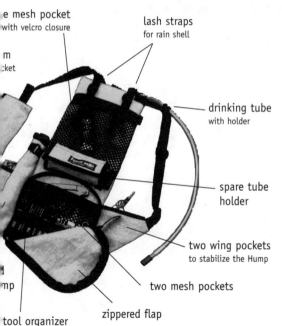

e mesh pocket
with velcro closure

m
cket

lash straps
for rain shell

drinking tube
with holder

spare tube
holder

two wing pockets
to stabilize the Hump

two mesh pockets

mp

zippered flap

tool organizer

This is not your ordinary, run-of-the-mill bladder bag. **The Forest Hump™** is the water and tool pack specifically designed with the mountain biker in mind! This incredibly light-weight pack not only carries everything you need, it also keeps it amazingly well organized—so you don't waste time fishing around. And it all stays secure on your back—even on your most insane downhill abuse sessions. You'll almost forget it's there! Available with 76 oz taste-free urethane bladder with extra-fat drinking tube.

grey/green or black	**$53**
with bladder	**$70**
Also Available:	
Forest HEmp	**$63**
with bladder	**$80**

Call Now To Order:
1-888-BEACHWAY

MOUNTAIN BIKE AMERI

series

The Mountain Bike America guidebook series is the cornerstone
Beachway Press' product line. This series of off-road bicycling guidebooks c
tures the heart and soul of one of the world's newest and most popular spc
with its innovative style, casual manner, comprehensive information, a
highly accurate maps using the latest in digital technology. The combinat
of these attributes makes each book within the series not only the prefer
source of information on where to ride in each area, but also the hallmark
guidebooks on this subject.

Give us a buzz or visit us on the web to learn about other current a
upcoming titles in this exciting and unique series.

... Enjoy Your World...

1-888-BEACHWAY